"If you are a woman, it will be toug
Smith's new book and not get mad

D1175147

WHAT YOUR DOCTOR DOESN'T WANT YOU TO KNOW *CAN* HURT YOU. . . .

THE MYTHS	THE FACTS
There are sound medical reasons for most hysterectomies.	Of the nearly six hundred thousand hysterectomies performed each year, nine out of ten are elective. That is, without medical imperative.
In-vitro fertilization is a viable alternative for infertile couples.	Success rates for in-vitro fertilization vary from less than 5% to near 20%, even in the major medical centers that specialize in this extraordinary therapy. Be skeptical of any local physician who claims to duplicate—or better—these success rates.
Only another doctor can request your files.	Your files—including test results, operative summaries, and pathology reports—belong to you. Beware of any doctor who refuses to provide you with copies.
D & C is the most effective treatment for abnormal bleeding.	Most dysfunctional bleeding is caused by the abnormal production of hormones by the brain. This condition is hormonally—not surgically—corrected.
Physician performance is monitored by the AMA.	Doctors are not monitored by the AMA, hospitals, or their peers. But with the help of this empowering book, they *can* be held accountable. . . .

WOMEN
and
DOCTORS

A Physician's Explosive Account of

Women's Medical Treatment—and

Mistreatment—in America Today

and What You Can Do About It

JOHN M. SMITH, M.D., FACOG

A Dell Trade Paperback

A DELL TRADE PAPERBACK

Published by
Dell Publishing
a division of
Bantam Doubleday Dell Publishing Group, Inc.
1540 Broadway
New York, New York 10036

ISBN: 0-440-50533-X

Reprinted by arrangement with The Atlantic Monthly Press

Printed in the United States of America

Published simultaneously in Canada

May 1993

10   9   8   7   6   5   4   3   2   1

BVG

TO MY WIFE, JANE RAGLE,

who has taught me so much:

how to see through the eyes of a woman,

what it takes to be a friend, and what it means to care.

I am richer because she is in my life.

ACKNOWLEDGMENTS

MY WARMEST THANKS TO FRIENDS AND FAMILY WHO GAVE ME SUPPORT AND encouragement to write this book. Without them, I might have given up on it. They include Gina Ragle, Jane Ragle, Alan Smith, Dr. William Smith, and Dr. Meredith Titus.

Thanks to my parents, Doris and Hugh Smith, for everything.

Thanks to my agent, Elizabeth Wales, for her help, and her insistence that I persist when it was not going well.

Thanks to my editor at Atlantic Monthly Press, Anton Mueller, for understanding the book so well, and for his expertise and help in the final shaping of it.

And special thanks to Carolyn Pelkey, whose remarkable competence made it so much easier than it might have been.

Finally, thanks to all the excellent doctors, nurses, and other health-care professionals who have shown me how *good* medical care can be.

CONTENTS

CONTENTS

CONTENTS

INTRODUCTION

THE HEALTH-CARE SYSTEM IN AMERICA IS FAILING. IT IS NO LONGER ABLE to meet the basic health needs of all Americans, and it is most especially unable to meet the needs of women. The medical profession has had a remarkable evolution, from a struggle for basic credibility in the early nineteenth century to an unparalleled level of authority and prestige today. Along the way, science and compassion have been blended with power and politics, and our modern health-care system is the result. There are many components to our system, but over time the medical profession has become the controlling force. Within that profession insensitivity, greed, and the arrogance of power have become all too commonplace. It is my opinion that the attitudes and behaviors of doctors are at the root of the problems that plague the health-care system. Those attitudes and behaviors are not the entire problem, as there are needed changes that lie outside the scope of physician behavior, but physician behavior is the essential element that must be changed if things are to get better.

Only very recently has there been a growing public awareness of how badly women are treated by their doctors and by the American health-care organization. Evidence brought to light reveals that medical research has been so slanted toward men that women are grossly misdiagnosed and inadequately or inappropriately treated for such disorders as heart disease, strokes, hypertension, lung cancer, and depression. The gender disparity in our system of medical research has been found to be so serious that the National Institutes of Health (NIH) announced in the fall of 1990 the establishment of the office of Research on Women's Health within the office of the Director of the NIH. Meanwhile, a tenured professor of neurosurgery, Dr. Frances Conley, publicly resigned from the faculty of the Stanford University School of Medicine because of the rampant sexism of her male colleagues. These "new revelations" come amid a background of "old news" about unnecessary hysterectomies and the continually rising rate of needless cesarean sections for childbirth. Much more remains unsaid.

Even though all consumers of medical care are adversely affected by what the health-care system as a whole has become, it is clear that women suffer most severely because they are at the hands of a specialty (gynecology) that is dominated by males, acting and thinking like males, and an entire system of medical research and treatment that has been shaped by males. A majority of women use a gynecologist as their source of primary medical care. Roughly 75 percent of these gynecologists are males. The consequences of this gender imbalance on women's health and well-being is still one of the least identified and discussed areas of needed health-care reform, though it is unquestionably the area of the most frequent and severe abuse.

In the last quarter century, women have indeed made progress toward reducing the abuse they suffer in their interaction with doctors. The development of a vital feminism in America has brought about some worthwhile changes, such as padded stirrups, speculum warmers, childbirth education, and a wider awareness of "patient's rights" in general. Nonetheless, the basic dynamics that create an abusive environment for women and the rising cost and declining availability of health care have not been changed enough.

*   *   *

The way we finance, deliver, and monitor health care must be revised so that adequate preventive care and treatment of illness are available to everyone on an equal basis, unaffected by affluence, influence, or gender. The necessary changes would be sweeping, but even if our nation has the political will to make these changes, it will not happen swiftly. While we wait, women are being abused by their physicians on a daily basis. For the immediate future, all women must become aware of the scope, nature, and cause of the problems and begin to protect themselves. All women must work toward changing the attitudes and practices of the physicians to whom they turn for care. They must also demand that the political and health-care financing systems begin to effectively change the behavior of all physicians, and all women must demand open access to the information about doctors and hospitals they need to make intelligent decisions about their health care. At present, this information is controlled by the medical profession, and is practically unavailable to women. This is but one of the ways in which doctors are able to maintain their dominance and autonomy.

At this point, many of you are saying "not my doctor, my doctor is honest, competent, and has only my welfare at heart." Please understand that a pleasant demeanor and impressive diplomas and certificates do not mean that your doctor is incapable of the behavior I will describe in this book. Regardless of your feelings about your current physician, it is worthwhile to at least step back, reassess, and ask yourself some pointed questions about your doctor and your relationship with him or her.

Let me assure you that this book is not meant to be an indictment of all physicians, or even all gynecologists. Not all doctors are insensitive, unskilled, mercenary, or uncaring. Many, however, are all of these things, and some are worse. Many unfortunate things happen to women at the hands of their physicians. These include unnecessary surgery, poorly done surgery, misinformation, prejudicial treatment, sexual abuse, and more. Recent studies document that various operations and other medical procedures are performed by American gynecologists at rates many times greater than in other industrialized countries. In my opinion, most of these are not only unnecessary but dangerous as well. Regardless of recent headline-making studies, relatively little has yet been published in medical journals about abuses by physicians. In general, the medical profession avoids anything that is critical of itself. Virtually nothing has been published that is available to readers of nonmedical literature.

It is critical that women be aware of the level of abuse occurring, that they have a healthy degree of sensitivity to it, that they understand what the appropriate relationship between them and their doctor should be, and that they learn to create the proper relationship with a given physician—or, if that's not possible, to recognize an improper doctor-patient relationship and end it quickly and decisively. Bringing you sufficient facts and ideas to enable you to do all of this for yourself, and making you indignant enough to demand action from others, is what this book is about.

I have relied on my own experience for much of the material in this book. After medical school, internship, and ob-gyn specialty training, I spent two years as an ob-gyn physician in the Air Force and then ten years in the private practice of obstetrics, gynecology, and infertility in Colorado Springs, Colorado. Doctors often dismiss critics by saying that they just haven't been there, in the front lines, and therefore have no right to criticize. I *have* been there, in the consultation room, in the operating room, in the delivery room, in the emergency room, in the calm of routine and the pressure of crisis. This personal experience as a practicing physician, knowing what constitutes good care and seeing abuse firsthand, is what creates the tone of immediacy in this book. That this tone can move toward anger and alarm is something I believe is warranted by the situation at hand.

In addition to my experience as a practicing physician, I was one of three founders of Peak Health Care, a company that developed, owned, and operated health-maintenance organizations (HMOs). We began the company in Colorado, took it public, then expanded into other states. In the course of developing all the HMOs, I had the opportunity to address, meet with, and question thousands of physicians in a dozen states. I also had the opportunity to review their billing practices and their approaches to the practice of medicine. From this experience I can say that, nationwide, the similarities among doctors far outweigh any differences, and the similarities among gynecologists are especially consistent. I believe that this is because gynecologists are almost all males, and the cultural indoctrination that stamps males with similar characteristics also brings about the unpleasant and unfortunate similarities in their behavior as doctors.

Needless to say, I have had to do a great deal of soul-searching and self-scrutinizing as a male gynecologist. I have also had to come to terms with my own past culpability. It has been a valuable part of the process of redefining myself as a male, something that all males, and especially male physicians, badly need to do. I have been incredibly fortunate to have a wife whose sensitive and sophisticated feminism has made her an ideal tutor. As I have struggled to free myself from my own apathy and ignorance and to genuinely understand the reality of the everyday discrimination experienced by women, she has played a vital role in my own redefinition. With the help of her perspective, my eyes have been further opened to what is experienced by a woman in the world of women's medical treatment.

Since publication of *Women and Doctors,* I have traveled throughout the country, and have enjoyed many radio, television, and bookstore appearances. The response from women has been overwhelmingly positive, and they have shared with me their own experiences with the medical profession. Their stories are powerfully consistent. I have long believed that the nature of women's experiences with their gynecologists is negative, even though their collective experience has never been quantified. If I had any doubt about the nature of that collective experience, it has been dispelled by the countless stories that women have told me.

The response by gynecologists has been less gratifying. A number of individual doctors have told me that they essentially agree with what I have written. Disappointingly, even some of the most competent and compassionate of these colleagues have expressed anger that I chose to publicly air the profession's shortcomings.

The response of the American College of Obstetrics and Gynecology, which is ultimately responsible for the training, certification, and representation of the nation's gynecologists, has been especially disappointing to me. Many writers and representatives of the electronic media contacted the College for comments about my book. The College refused to comment, but, curiously, often added that they disagreed with some of my statistics. Finally, pressed by a newspaper reporter, they listed the numbers with which they disagreed. With one exception, all were numbers I had obtained from the American College itself, though a year or so earlier. Even though the statistics had changed in the interim, the changes were insignificant. In this edition, I have changed those numbers, and must assume that nothing remains in this book with which the American College of Obstetrics and Gynecology is willing, or able, to take issue.

Unfortunately, the American gynecologic establishment is also unwilling to admit that serious problems exist within the profession, and that women are suffering the consequences of those problems. I would like to see nationwide surveys performed that would quantify such things as the level of dissatisfaction that women feel about their medical treatment and the frequency with which women experience sexual molestation by their gynecologists. I would like to see anonymous surveys of nurses who work in the ob-gyn setting, designed to measure the frequency with which they witness inappropriate or incompetent behavior by doctors; and I would like to see data gathered directly from patients about their actual experiences with the pain, complications, and sequelae of hysterectomy and C-sections.

I would not want the American College of Obstetrics and Gynecology to conduct such surveys and studies; the potential conflicts of interest are too great. Rather, the gathering of this data should be the responsibility of the government. It would be entirely appropriate that such activity be included as part of the women's health initiative recently funded within the National Institutes of Health.

No matter how widely *Women and Doctors* is read, there will be no sweeping change from the medical profession until there is a public demonstration of the widespread dissatisfaction that unquestionably exists among women about their medical treatment. My hope is to provoke the studies necessary to provide documentation that cannot be denied.

* * *

This book is arranged in four sections. The first is intended to give you a clear sense of the problems that exist, both on a national scale and for you as a patient.

The second is composed of stories of real patients who have come to harm at the hands of real gynecologists. My intention in this section is to bring home the reality of the threat that exists and to help you to understand that every woman is at risk. I am aware that in the past some excellent books have helped raise the consciousness of women concerning their rights as patients. In spite of the high quality of many of these books, an appropriate degree of alarm has not yet been sounded. Perhaps the only way to convey the hard realities of the situation is to tell real stories of real women.

In the third section I have provided information about how physicians are trained, licensed, and given hospital privileges, and I have described the alternatives to receiving care from gynecologists or other M.D.s. The section ends with suggestions about how to find the right health-care provider and how to form the appropriate relationship with him or her. Finding the right doctor is the first step toward ensuring that you have the possibility of receiving the best care. Creating a relationship that fosters the right attitude and approach is the next.

In the last section, I have provided a directory of basic information about the most common gynecological problems, along with advice about how to deal with physicians regarding these problems. The section includes specific questions to ask a doctor about each of these problem areas. It is as up-to-date as I can make it, and I hope you will be able to use it as a reference for some time to come.

In the Epilogue, I move beyond the problems of women's health care and address the problem of health care in general: the two areas are inextricably related.

If this book fulfills its purpose you will approach the health-care setting with an appropriate level of suspicion and a healthy level of cynicism, and you will be sufficiently empowered to protect yourself from harm and to see to it that your needs are met.

SECTION ONE

The Health-Care Problem for Women and America

One

WOMEN IN THE CONTEXT OF THE NATIONAL PICTURE

THE PROBLEMS WOMEN EXPERIENCE IN THE HEALTH-CARE SYSTEM REFLECT the problems of the system in general. Women, however, are impacted on a scale that is disproportionate to their numbers. Whether you are talking about unnecessary surgery, inappropriate treatment or testing, lack of preventive care, lack of consideration in research, allocation of dollars, or simply being milked for dollars by physicians, women are mistreated on a major scale. They experience these abuses far more frequently than their male counterparts, regardless of economic or work status or any other factor. Gender alone is the determinant.

The United States Office of Management and Budget tells us that we spent approximately 675 *billion* dollars in 1990 on what we call health care. If nothing is done to change the way we control our system, this amount is expected to rise to a *trillion* dollars by the year 2000. In the past five years, the amount spent for each person has tripled, to over $2,500 for every man, woman, and child. In spite of this staggering amount of money, we get far less health "care" than we need and far more medical "treatment," while many Americans receive neither good health care nor appropriate medical treatment.

If the problem were static things would be bad enough. In fact, the problem is worsening in every possible way. As costs steadily and exponentially increase, more and more Americans have no health-care insurance coverage. As the cost of providing coverage to employees increases, businesses founder under the weight of the ever-expanding portion of their expenses that must be allocated for this purpose. Government officials, from the Secretary of Health and Human Services to growing numbers of congressional representatives, have used the word "crisis" to describe the situation, a label that usually precedes dramatic legislation. In this case, however, we are seeing government planning moves that will inevitably make matters worse, because they constitute the same basic errors that created the mess in the first place. They simply don't understand the dynamics of the problem in general, and the problem for women in particular is being given the same lack of attention that the male-dominated government has shown for women's problems in the past. Women with children constitute the largest and fastest-growing group below the poverty line, and as such are disproportionately affected by government cutbacks in services. Men in government seem unable to grasp the consequences of their actions on this portion of society, which often appears to them to be invisible. To quote Representative Patricia Schroeder, "they just don't get it."

Politicians also seem to have failed to grasp the wisdom in the definition of insanity I recall as attributed to Einstein, that being when you repeat the same process over and over and expect a different result.

Because our legislators have been led away from an understanding of the magnitude of the role of physician behavior in health-care cost escalation, all their efforts have centered on trying to simply limit payment to physicians and hospitals for services under those plans that the government administers. As a result, fewer and fewer Medicaid and Medicare recipients find doctors and hospitals willing to provide services for them. We thus have a set of government programs that progressively cut out of the system the very people it was intended to cover. For those who somehow manage to receive care within this framework a different standard of care has evolved, causing the poor and elderly to be victims of the same sorts of discrimination in treatment that women have always experienced.

In addition to discouraging physicians from seeing Medicaid and Medicare recipients, government programs have had a negative ripple effect in many other areas. Combined with an overall system that gives physicians the wrong incentives, these programs have resulted in massive waste that has nothing to do with the absolute cost of a given procedure or service.

Studies by Professional Review Organizations (PROs), HMOs, and other organizations have shown that more than half of all laboratory tests performed on patients in America are worthless. It's important to know that this is true only in America. Other modern countries around the world exhibit no such excesses. At least half of all the days that patients spend in hospitals are useless, either because the treatment itself is unnecessary or because the treatment could be provided in a different, and less costly, setting. There is no adequate provision whatever for the long-term treatment of the elderly or the chronically disabled in a setting that is both affordable and that meets the emotional and medical needs of these patients.

We have no mechanism, as a nation, to make decisions about the allocation of limited medical resources and money. Even if we did, we would then have no way to ensure that these decisions are carried into effect in the treatment setting. As a result, individuals, insurance companies, and the government lose vast sums of money paying for useless and/or unwanted medical treatment for the terminally ill. Secretary of Health and Human Services Louis Sullivan, speaking in Detroit in September 1991, said "costs are rising at an unsustainable rate." That was an obvious conclusion, coming just after the government reported that spending on health care had risen 10.5 percent in 1990, the third consecutive year of a double-digit increase. But he went on to say that "the American people will not—and should not—accept radical departures from a system that offers them so much." In other words, don't expect creative and dramatic leadership from Washington.

While nothing fruitful is accomplished at the government level, women can and must attack the problems as they exist in their corner of this large arena. Understanding that the faults do not lie with technology, law, or financial systems but rather with human behavior is the first step to effecting change.

Two

THE EXPERIENCE FOR WOMEN IN THE SYSTEM

THE USUAL EXPERIENCE FOR A WOMAN GOING TO A GYNE-cologist includes humiliation, depersonalization, even pain, and too seldom does she come away with her needs having been met. Some of this is inevitable, because it's not easy for anyone to be a patient. The role tends to mean vulnerability, lack of control, and a degree of physical and emotional exposure that is hard to tolerate even in a relationship with a friend or relative, much less with a physician who is neither. Simply bestowing the title of "Doctor" on someone creates an aura of superiority that can make even the most mature and competent woman feel unequal and insecure, and when a physician *acts* like "Doctor," it makes an appropriate relationship impossible.

According to the American College of Obstetrics and Gynecology, about two-thirds of women go to a gynecologist for their primary care. This means that they take to their gynecologist's office all their needs—for information, for reassurance, for health screening, for treatment of disease, for help with problems in their marriages, their sexuality, their lives. Few gynecologists know about, or care about, most of these things, so few women are helped by them to live more happily or to feel more well. Even fewer come away from the physician encounter feeling better than when they went in. Many of them come away having been harmed.

In 1991, nearly 600,000 hysterectomies were performed in America. That's about one every 50 seconds! I suppose that fact alone will not necessarily astonish you, but it should astonish you to know that more than nine out of ten of those operations are *elective* procedures. That means that there is no medical imperative that the hysterectomy be done; that if it is not done, nothing dire will result. It is my personal estimation that over half of the hysterectomies that are performed are not only elective, but have no reasonable justification at all. Still, one-third of all American women will have had their uterus removed by the time they reach age sixty.

It is a sad fact that shabby treatment, uncalled-for testing, and unnecessary surgery are experienced by people of all ages, classes, races, and gender, but it is also a fact that women are treated differently from others by health-care providers *simply because they are women.*

In December 1990, the American Medical Association Council on Ethical and Judicial Affairs adopted a report, the title of which was "Gender Disparities in Clinical Decision-Making." This report was the result of the evaluation of forty-eight studies concerning whether a person's sex inappropriately affects the amounts and kinds of medical treatment they receive.

The summary of their conclusions deserves to be quoted. It states:

> These studies have documented gender disparities in treatment in a number of areas, including kidney transplantation, cardiac catheterization and the diagnosis of lung cancer. While biological factors account for some differences between the sexes in the delivery of medical care, the studies indicate that there may be non-biological or non-clinical factors which affect clinical decision-making. There are not enough data to identify the exact nature of the non-biological or non-clinical

factors. Nevertheless, their existence is a cause for concern that needs to be addressed by the medical community.

The Council on Ethical and Judicial Affairs recommends that physicians examine their practices and attitudes for influence of social or cultural biases which could be inadvertently affecting the delivery of medical care. The nature of any biological or non-clinical factors which affect the delivery of medical care should be ascertained, and any inappropriate biases eliminated. In addition, more research in women's health issues and women's health problems should be pursued. Finally, awareness of and responsiveness to sociocultural factors which could lead to gender disparities may be enhanced by increasing the number of female physicians in leadership roles and other positions of authority in teaching, research, and the practice of medicine.

My experience with the AMA leads me to conclude that if they were willing to adopt this report (and thereby validate it), the significance of the findings are surely worse than they stated. I'm not aware of publicity concerning this report at the time it was written, but all the studies on which it was based had previously been published in medical journals. The AMA's reason for existence is not to apprise the public of the shortcomings of physicians, but rather to enhance their public image and maintain their power, control, and affluence. This they have historically done very well. The medical lobby as a whole, the largest unit of which is that of the AMA, is incredibly effective. Recently, the government concluded a massive study of physician reimbursement. Congress, acting on the resulting recommendations, authorized sweeping changes in Medicare and Medicaid payment schedules for physicians. The medical lobby went to work and convinced Congress to undo this reform measure on the basis that paying doctors less would result in poorer health for Americans. I have been told by legislative aides to senators that Congress is easily influenced by this lobby group and generally buys whatever arguments it produces.

In fairness, I must applaud the AMA for adopting the report that came out of this study, and I take it as a positive sign for the future. The reporting committee actually reviewed forty-eight studies that had been published in various medical journals between 1970 and 1990. Some of the findings in those studies, though they got essentially no press at the time of their publication, have made national headlines lately and contributed to the NIH's decision to open its new office of Women's Health. Other significant findings have not received much public attention. Studies that have received wide publicity as well as those known only to readers of medical literature, though, validate my personal experience and observations, and document the reality of gender inequity in health care.

One study documented that females with severe enough kidney disease to require dialysis were 30 percent less likely to receive a kidney transplant than were males. Another study put that difference at 25 percent. In addition, men in every age category were more likely than women to receive a transplant.

Even though men and women smokers are at identical risk for the development of lung cancer, studies showed that men were twice as likely to have appropriate tests ordered to determine if they had the disease.

In the area of heart disease, a study done in 1987 determined that men have cardiac catheterizations ordered at a rate disproportionately higher than women, regardless of the fact that both sexes are at equal risk for coronary-artery disease. When men and women who had received nuclear-scan heart tests were reviewed, pure prejudice showed up in the findings. Of those patients with abnormal test results, women were more than twice as likely to have their symptoms attributed to somatic, psychiatric, or other noncardiac causes. Of the women with normal tests, those who were most likely to actually have heart disease were also the most likely to have their symptoms attributed to a noncardiac cause.

In 1985 the Public Health Service's Task Force on Women's Health Issues reported that the lack of research data on women limited understanding of women's health needs. It is now widely recognized that medical research has been grossly slanted toward male models, and that much of the medical treatment of women has been based on that research. It is also now widely recognized that women may react differently than men to a treatment and that some diseases manifest themselves differently in women. It seems to have taken two centuries for the American medical profession to notice that women are different from men!

The gender bias in research subjects has created serious problems in the diagnosis and treatment of women in such areas as cardiovascular disease, alcoholism, drug dependency, and mental illness. In addition, many areas of medication prescribing in which the effects of medication vary with sex have been researched using only men as clinical subjects.

This is all only the tip of the iceberg. It is bad enough that over a long period of time prejudice has resulted in gender bias in research. In the context of an individual male gynecologist diagnosing and treating an individual woman right now, gender prejudice results in much more immediate and pronounced harm. In the section titled "Real Patients, Real Stories," you will see what those prejudices can mean to you in any given encounter with your gynecologist.

Three

THE BEHAVIOR OF DOCTORS IN GENERAL

IT IS CRITICAL TO REALIZE THAT PHYSICIANS ARE JUST PEOPLE, WITH THE same potential for good and bad behavior as any other group. It has been shown time and again that human beings given power over other human beings will abuse it. Physicians, unfortunately, have created for themselves an inappropriate societal role and status that includes a high degree of power and authority. Medicine men and priests may have wielded such power in long-ago cultures. The power physicians enjoy in our contemporary culture is greater than that of any other industrialized society, or at any other point in modern time. Some doctors have responded much as you would predict, with intentional abuse of that power and authority. These doctors may be in the minority, but they are surely dangerous.

Most doctors, however, are not consciously mercenary, dishonest, or hurtful. They live in their own subculture, which reinforces their self-image as totally honest, well-meaning, caring, and special members of society. Many doctors regularly abuse women as a result of underlying prejudice and self-deception. They have concluded honestly, though mistakenly, that they occupy a special niche that should be unchallenged, and that they possess a valid body of knowledge that allows them to heal without harm.

Doctors who do unnecessary operations on women almost always genuinely believe that they are acting in the best interest of the women. Because their behavior is not the result of a conscious decision to do harm, but rather the result of psychosocial conditioning that leads to the behavior, we cannot simply ferret out the bad guys and eliminate them. We actually have to change the ways doctors are taught, socialized, conditioned, and reinforced. Doctors weren't born as they are; we, the consumers of medical care, have ourselves to blame for their "creation."

No other professional in America enjoys the degree of authority that physicians have managed to secure. Almost unquestioned in their judgments, they have been given the authority to exercise power in areas that extend beyond their medical area of competence. A physician can decide if a person is to be incarcerated in a mental hospital against his or her will, or whether a person is considered legally sane or mentally incompetent. They can even decide, after a person has died, if that person was sane when his or her will was written.

Physicians can also decide if you should be allowed to do certain kinds of work or if you can play a sport in school, and can exercise unquestioned power in myriad other aspects of your life. Within the medical setting, they completely control the flow of information to a patient, and the patient has little opportunity to verify the accuracy of that information. They also control the flow of money in the health-care system, and not a dollar is spent without their authorization. This occurs because nothing can be done to a patient without an order from a licensed physician.

They control not only how much money is spent, but also who gets it. This is true because only physicians are licensed by a state to practice medicine. Hospitals aren't, nursing homes aren't, insurance companies aren't, and the government isn't. Regardless of who is responsible for *paying* for a medical test, procedure, drug, or time in a hospital bed, these things cannot be done without an order written by a licensed physician.

While physicians have unparalleled authority, they also have almost complete autonomy. Physicians have been able to safeguard the ability to set their own fees, and to effectively squelch competition. As positive systems of competition and quality control have been introduced, the nation's physicians have created new ways to retain their control and to maintain the flow of dollars to themselves. While various agencies have tried to introduce systems of effective review of medical practices, the nation's physicians have stonewalled the effort and have become more and more unwilling to have their patients know as much as they deserve to know about their own care. They have almost universally refused to participate in meaningful review procedures and have, through their various organizations, effectively blocked efforts to make public details about their training, fees, C-section and complication rates, malpractice-suit experience, and the frequency and nature of complaints filed against them with State Boards of Medical Examiners.

The opportunity for incompetence, shabby workmanship, or even charlatanism is maintained by the secrecy that the medical profession demands, always with the claim that physicians are above reproach and are the only professionals who deserve to be free from real scrutiny. We don't allow totally unmonitored activity by our engineers, builders, or anyone else; why do we allow it for those who work on our bodies?

Perhaps part of the problem is that most people don't realize that real scrutiny of physicians is not occurring. They read about government Professional Review Organizations, hospital audits, and peer-review procedures and believe that physicians must be closely watched. As a physician, I can tell you unequivocally that it is not the case.

Real peer review, in which physicians evaluate and critique other physicians, does not exist. There have been many attempts to get the medical profession to "police itself" in this way, but doctors absolutely refuse to participate. My personal experience in setting up utilization-review and quality-assurance systems in HMOs may shed some light here. What I discovered was that doctors would go along with the program as long as I did not ask them to actually participate in evaluating the practices of other physicians, and as long as whatever data was accumulated concerning individual physicians' medical behavior was not made available to patients.

It is part of the largely unspoken agreement among physicians that they will maintain the integrity of the "fraternity" against all outsiders by not giving potentially negative information to anyone outside the group. A good example of this is their refusal, almost universally, to testify against other physicians in malpractice litigation. It extends, however, to the most unthreatening of processes, such as quality-assurance programs, as well as to potentially lethal situations, such as when physicians fail to notify authorities of drug or alcohol abuse, mental aberration, or gross incompetence by other physicians.

Doctors on hospital staffs are organized into "sections" by specialty (gynecology, surgery, pediatrics, internal medicine, and so on). These sections are required by federal regulation to perform "audits" designed to evaluate the quality of care in the hospital and to discern problem areas and problem physicians. In reality, these studies are usually put together by the medical records librarian and are always designed so that they cannot possibly identify bad practice. It is the doctors themselves, after all, who interpret the data, and I have never seen a group of doctors indict themselves.

The procedure usually goes like this: At a meeting of, say, the ob-gyn section the doctors are told that an audit is due by the standards of the American Hospital Association. The doctors ask what kind of audit has to be done and are told that it needs to be something about, for example, the adequacy of the preoperative records. After discussion, the doctors decide to have the medical-

records people count the number of patients that have had hysterectomies without a recent Pap smear being documented in their
charts. A few weeks later, they receive a report that tells them that
20 percent of the charts were deficient in this way. They decide to
send out a letter to all the gynecologists on the staff telling them to
be sure to document for the record that their patients have had Pap
smears prior to a hysterectomy. Over the course of the next year,
the process is monitored by medical records and reported again. As
a result, the charts get "doctored," but nothing significant about
patient care has been altered. In this case, there would be no attempt
to determine whether a specific doctor has been taking out uteruses
without first determining if the patient had cancer. The point was
only to determine if the doctor dictated "Pap smear in December
was negative" in the admission history and physical.

I have only once seen a physician section take action to remove a doctor from the staff because of incompetence. That occurred because the surgeon, who had a history of surgical complications and questions of competence, had a surgical error result in the
death of a relative of one of the hospital employees while a number
of other employees looked on. The rest of the surgeons succumbed
to the threat of having the hospital employee staff boycott them if
they did not act. The surgeon then simply moved to another state to
practice. That is what usually happens when it becomes public
knowledge that a doctor has a serious problem. The state he is
leaving is usually so happy for him to go that they don't risk telling
the state where he is moving about his problems, so his problems
continue, only somewhere else.

Doctors need to do very little finagling to keep their office
behavior secret. The records, written by the doctors themselves, are
the property of the individual physician and cannot be looked into
by any government agency, review organization, or insurance company without the doctor's permission and assistance. True, a patient

has a right to see her records, but she usually must request them in writing, and many physicians will initially tell a patient that they will only send the records to another physician. If the patient requests that they be sent to an attorney, physicians will notify their malpractice-insurance carriers, require the attorney to pay for copying, and often "edit" the material before it is sent. Even if unedited, it often arrives in an unordered pile, frequently with selected pieces missing.

In the midst of this atmosphere of total authority, autonomy, and control of information, physicians can easily get away with anything. Moreover, our system of paying for their services provides them with incentives to do the wrong things, while creating little in the way of disincentives for doing bad things. Our system, in short, directs that the more doctors *do* to a patient, the more money they make, and we let the doctors (acting alone, virtually in secret) decide what to do. Doctors have effectively convinced the public that any effort, on anyone's part, to monitor what they do would result in jeopardy to "quality of care." The truth is, when you boil down all the considerations, facts, and figures, the *less* that is done to you, the healthier you will be. We traditionally have not paid doctors to keep us healthy, we have paid them to *do* things to us, and they continue to fight to protect their opportunity to do those things, whether they are in our best interests or not.

They have obviously done a good job of exploiting the opportunity. In spite of massive efforts to control health-care costs, physician income has consistently risen at a rate greater than the cost-of-living index, and greater even than the medical component of that same index. Physicians' average net income was $113,192 in 1970 and rose to $132,300 by 1987. In 1988 and '89 it grew by 9 percent and 8 percent, respectively. While we have decried the predominance of greed in our culture in the 1980s, we have focused on bankers, brokers, and developers as epitomizing this sign of societal sickness. Why have we ignored the behavior of physicians and failed to label the same behavior as what it really is? What can you call it but greed when an ophthalmologist charges $3,000 to perform a cataract procedure that takes twenty minutes? Doctors have too long been able to label their own behavior for the public, and it's time we shined a bright light on it and defined it for ourselves.

It was natural that physicians should come under greater scrutiny. The steadily growing public awareness and unhappiness about the cost of health care and the dissatisfaction with its quality and availability made that all but inevitable—especially since, unlike doctors, the average American worker doesn't have the opportunity to enjoy a large income while making a bad product. The ratio of physician income in America relative to the average compensation of all workers in 1986 was 5.1 to 1. In West Germany that ratio was 4 to 3, in Canada, 3 to 7, in Japan, 2 to 5, and in the United Kingdom, 2 to 4. Interestingly, hysterectomies are performed in the United Kingdom with a frequency that is one-third the rate in the United States.

Perhaps the income of corporate CEOs has grown faster than that of American doctors. In general, however, corporate CEOs are rewarded for the creation of value, such as increased production capability, stockholder wealth, and new product development. What value has been created by our doctors that justifies their making more money than physicians in any other country? You would be hard-pressed to find any measure by which we seem to be getting what we pay for. The U.S. infant-mortality rate, at 10 deaths per 1,000 births, is lower than ever, but it ranks twenty-second among industrialized nations. Japan is first with 4.4 per 1,000, and the rate in Canada (whose per capita expenditure on health care is half that of the United States) is 7.9. Our maternal-mortality rate is

8.0 per 100,000 live births, while that of Canada is 3.2. In spite of this, the medical profession in America continues to convince Congress that reducing doctors' incomes would jeopardize the health of U.S. citizens.

Four

THE MISCASTING OF MALES AS GYNECOLOGISTS

THERE IS IN OUR CULTURE A UNIFORM ENCULTURIZATION OF MALES. Women historically had a similar uniform experience that defined them, but since the beginning of the feminist movement this has changed dramatically. Women have actively tried to redefine themselves, as they want to be and believe they are, rather than accepting the definition that our society, and males, have imposed upon them. Men have not significantly done this. As a group, they are at least twenty-five years behind women in declaring that they will no longer accept the necessity, validity, or value of all males being trained to play "traditional" male roles.

Meanwhile, however, the specialty of obstetrics-gynecology is dominated by males who act and think as males are trained to act and think in American culture. What are the common messages that American males carry into adulthood and American gynecologists bring to the role of "caring" for women?

We learn to be anything but "female"—that is, we should not experience, much less show, feelings of tenderness, compassion, sensitivity, or vulnerability. "Real men" dominate rather than co-operate, control rather than nurture, own rather than share. These attributes pervade every aspect of our lives but are nowhere more apparent than in our relationships with women. We learn at an early age that women are weak and in need of our protection, and that they exist for our pleasure, the taking of which should be under our control and direction. Many males may also suspect that if the relationship were altered women would discover our many inadequacies. Most adult males are unable to eliminate much of this from their relationships with women, and male gynecologists are no different. They bring their male prejudice against females and their need to be dominating and controlling to the doctor-patient relationship.

The consequence of gynecologists bringing their maleness to their relationships with their patients is that they don't really comprehend women's needs, don't respect their body integrity, don't regard or understand their values, and can't relate to their sexuality. They cannot truly empathize with women, nor can they identify with them in a meaningful way. In short, I believe that men have no business being gynecologists, certainly not men who are not significantly different from other men in their attitudes and prejudices about women. I have come to this opinion gradually, and not easily. I *am* a male gynecologist, and it has been hard for me to accept as truth the inherent shortcomings of males in this role. But the truth of it is supported by my own experience with the profession, by the collective experience of women as patients, and by a substantial body of medical studies, some of which I described in Chapter Two.

One of the conclusions of the AMA report of the Council on Ethical and Judicial Affairs was that

> Gender bias may not necessarily manifest itself as overt discrimination based on sex. Rather, social attitudes, including stereotypes, prejudices, and other evaluations based on gender roles may play themselves out in a variety of subtle ways.
>
> For instance, there is evidence that physicians are more likely to perceive women's maladies than men's as the result of

emotionality. Also, many researchers have noted the greater utilization of health care services by women than men and have attributed this difference to "overanxiousness" or *over-utilization* on the part of women without supporting evidence.

In other words, the prejudice is there, and it is real, and it means that women are treated differently by male physicians.

Male gynecologists, like all men, go through the kind of "attitude setting" that occurs in the proverbial locker rooms while they are growing into manhood. And this legacy carries on. It is common and acceptable among practicing gynecologists to speak about their patients and their patients' bodies, sexual behavior, or medical problems indiscriminately, in terms that are demeaning and reflect a lack of simple kindness and respect. Some of this is learned in those years of specialty training, where exposure to higher-level residents and staff sets the standards of behavior, and where the ways of relating to and thinking about women as patients are taught by example. The most distressing omission in this learning experience is that empathy, compassion, and sensitivity are seldom exhibited or taught along with the teaching of technical and intellectual skills. All the old male stereotypical thinking about women is reinforced in these males, who are supposed to be unique in their ability to relate to, understand, and care for women.

I would give a lot to be able to share with you my experiences in watching gynecologists' behavior when their patients are not around or have been rendered helpless and unconscious for surgical procedures. I have had a colleague invite me to do an exam on one of his patients under the false guise of a consultation because "she has a body you won't believe." I've seen a physician walk out of an exam room and tell a hallway full of doctors and nurses about the disease his married patient had contracted as a result of an affair. I have seen more than one gynecologist walk into an operating room where another doctor's patient was already asleep for surgery, lift up the sheet, admire the patient's breasts, and continue his conversation without pause.

Almost everyone is familiar with the ways that men tend to view and speak about rape and rape victims. The examples used to demonstrate that this particularly insensitive instance of sexism is alive and well are usually quotes from the judges, lawyers, or policemen involved with rape trials. I am sorry to tell you that the same language, reflecting the same attitudes, is commonly used by gynecologists.

In teaching hospitals, it is quite common for a gynecologic intern or resident to be called to the emergency room to do an examination of a sexual-assault victim, most often at the request of the police. In my training years, I virtually never heard these women referred to as anything but a "rape case." The attendant conversation was always replete with the same meanness, prejudice, and stupidity: "the stupid bitch was walking alone at two o'clock," or "you should have seen this one, miniskirt, no bra, she was asking for it," or "it wasn't a real rape, she was a hooker." Unfortunately, I continued to hear the same sort of thing from private-practice gynecologists in later years. The only time it varied significantly was if the victim was one of the doctor's affluent patients, was physically harmed, and presented no "mitigating" elements, such as being a heavy drinker or having had an affair or a sexually transmitted disease, making her suspect in his mind as to her guilt in the event.

I could recite a mind-boggling litany of such stories, but it would serve no further purpose. The point is that when you are not watching, doctors do not behave as you would like them to behave and, as you know, many don't behave as you would like even when you are.

The relationship between a woman and her physician implies a great deal of trust. She exposes her body, her emotions, her sexuality, because she needs the skills that the doctor has to offer. To treat this woman with anything less than complete respect, to reveal her confidences, to reduce her dignity, or to abuse the privileged access to her body is a totally unacceptable betrayal, a violation of trust. Few women would accept this kind of abusive behavior from a friend or lover, but many apparently feel that they have no choice but to accept it from a physician.

Women don't have to accept things as they are. Women must assume leadership in the role of physicians to women, and displace men from the majority and dominance in that role. It is a rare male who is able to see women day in and day out, examine their bodies, hear the details of their sex lives, and not only never have a lascivious thought or abuse that access but always remain clinical and objective, yet caring and empathetic. It would be a rare woman who could abuse that relationship. Much in gynecologic residency is dehumanizing, and much creates a sameness of perspective among graduates. Women, though, should be able to come through it without losing their empathy with women, and thus be able to serve other women's needs far better than men can.

After twenty-four years of medical education and clinical gynecological experience, it is my opinion that males should not be gynecologists. The role properly belongs to women. Not only are they the only sex truly able to understand, empathize with, and appropriately relate to women in the already difficult doctor-patient relationship, but isn't it true that, given a choice, almost every woman would prefer to see a woman gynecologist? Women gynecologists might still act like other doctors in the areas that relate to income generation, but I believe they are incapable of inflicting the level of harm to other women that is now inflicted by males. In the remainder of the book I'll try to convince you further of this view, as well as to give you my ideas of how to bring about change and how to cope with the situation you face in the meanwhile.

As you read, please remember that I do not mean to say that *no* male physician is capable of being as sensitive and compassionate as a woman, only that women as a group are better candidates than men as a group to act as primary-care physicians for women. Even though obstetrics and gynecology is not, as it currently exists, a true primary-care specialty, it is a specialty that is just beginning to be dominated by women. This year 54 percent of first-year residents in ob-gyn training programs are women. It will take some years before their influence is sufficient to change the nature of the specialty.

Five

WOMEN EFFECTING CHANGE

FOR THE LAST TWENTY-FIVE YEARS WOMEN HAVE BEEN CHANGING THEIR definition of themselves and their role in society, though admirable feminists existed long before the feminist movement gained wide recognition. Feminists' primary goal has been gender equity in all areas of our culture. Each time a milestone is reached, they set their sights on the next level, and continue to do a remarkable job of bringing about dramatic change.

Part of the feminist agenda has already begun to deal with some of the issues involved in women's health care. Such books as *Our Bodies, Ourselves* empowered a generation of women to demand fundamental changes in the way they were treated in the health-care setting. In the 1970s and 1980s women's awareness concerning their rights as patients was raised significantly. I feel strongly that it is time for women to set their sights on the next level.

As the previously quoted AMA report documented, there is significant prejudice in the world of medicine, and it affects women profoundly. That study found not only the existence of prejudicial attitudes but that this prejudice results in such inequities as women being less likely to receive a kidney transplant, less likely to have their lung cancer diagnosed, and less likely to have cardiac catheterization ordered when symptoms indicate it. Medical research has historically been structured around males, and resulting diagnostic and treatment models are often inappropriate for women. These things occur, apparently, because of the perceptions, attitudes, and biases about women in the minds of the males who dominate all aspects of health-care research and treatment.

None of the treatment discrepancies evaluated in the reports I have quoted concern diseases unique to women. When the same kinds of discrimination are applied in the arena of gynecology, the results are dramatically worse. We have not yet looked closely enough at it, been public enough and honest enough about it, and until that happens, nothing will change.

There are many parallel situations that women have actively addressed, and in addressing have begun to change. Ten years ago "acquaintance rape" was not in the national vocabulary. People didn't know it existed. It did, of course, and now that it has been brought under scrutiny and called by name, change is beginning to occur. The same thing needs to happen with women's medical treatment. An unindicated hysterectomy is an assault, but no doctor is ever charged with a crime for doing it. What do you call it if a doctor subjects your daughter to a breast and pelvic exam when there is no medical indication for it and your daughter didn't ask for it? Is it any less a sexual assault than her being fondled and disrobed by a date who thinks he "has the right"?

In recent years we have recognized that the seduction of a woman by her psychiatrist is, in fact, a criminal act. Similar abuse occurs in the gynecological setting but is called something else. Perhaps because women have not felt sufficiently empowered to threaten gynecologists' positions, these doctors have not been subjected to the same level of scrutiny as other professionals. It is time to hold them accountable.

* * *

We have seen the beginnings of change. There is now a broad public discussion about rape and widespread effort to address the situation. On college campuses males are being educated and reoriented about their own sexual behavior, the vulnerability of women, and communication between the sexes. There is also the beginning of public acknowledgment that gender inequities exist in the health-care system. There has been the public disclosure that a female physician in a prestigious medical center was subjected to the humiliation of sexual prejudice by male physicians. The terms "rocket scientist" and "brain surgeon" have become metaphors in our language for the best and brightest: I don't know if any female rocket scientists have been pinched, patted, and patronized, but we now know that a female brain surgeon at the Stanford Medical Center was not spared such indignities by her male medical colleagues. If you send a sexist to medical school, you can only wind up with a sexist doctor. Nothing in the academic medical environment results in the restructuring of male attitudes and prejudices, and that must change.

Awareness of gender inequity in medical care has been slow in developing. But public awareness has not yet begun to broach the real causes, or the actual severity, of the problem and certainly hasn't begun to produce a better health-care environment for women. For those things to occur, there has to be a shift in control of women's medical care toward women (at the present, only 25 percent of Fellows of the American College of Obstetrics and Gynecology are female), and the men who are currently the majority of women's doctors have to undergo serious attitude retraining and behavior modification.

Beginning now, every woman needs to approach her encounters with physicians and the health-care system with a new eye. The critical thing, as it has been in the other areas of the women's movement, is to be acutely aware of reality. If a woman can't see and accurately label sex discrimination in the workplace, she cannot begin to change it. If she cannot see and label abuse in the doctor's office, it will continue.

In the remainder of the book, I hope to show you what is really going on out there. Read it with an open mind. The stories of patients are absolutely true, unexaggerated, and as likely to happen to you as to the women described. Believe it, and you will be on the way to creating change. I have no quick fix for you, but I have some suggestions that will be helpful and may save your life, and some information and advice that will give you more control over the situation should you actually need treatment.

I will also describe the alternatives that may exist for you as an individual right now, and will describe the changes that I feel should be sought. Assuming that you agree, you can then begin to act as an agent for reform. I have seen no more powerful a catalyst for change in our society than the concerted action of women, and I would like nothing more than to see it now directed to the issue of abuse in the medical treatment of women.

Real Patients,
Real Stories

INTRODUCTION

IN THE FIRST SECTION I DISCUSSED THE GENERAL ISSUES CONCERNING HOW the health-care system impacts women as a group, and I largely used studies and data that are generally available. This section will move on to my personal experience.

Twenty years of experience with the medical profession has shaped my perceptions and feelings. Those twenty years include four years of medical school, a year of internship, three years of gynecologic residency, two years of military service as an obstetrician-gynecologist, and ten years of private practice. That same period includes the seven years in which I was simultaneously developing the health-care systems for our HMO company.

Twenty years in medicine adds up to countless encounters with patients, and countless opportunities to observe doctors at work. The experiences that I will recount in this section are examples of the things that have, in large part, motivated me to write this book. They are but a few of the many experiences that aroused deep feelings of anger in me. In reading them, I expect, you will experience anger as well, and I think it is important that I don't misdirect that anger.

There are many kinds of doctors in America, and they represent as many types of people as are represented in any other group. Some are bad doctors, who have poor skills, make mistakes, and hurt women through incompetence. Some are bad people, who use women patients to make money or for other self-serving reasons. The majority are neither of these. Most women's doctors are basically good people who possess adequate knowledge and skill and feel that they are always acting in the best interests of their patients. But even these doctors frequently, though unintentionally, exhibit behavior and attitudes that are abusive to their patients. Some of these practices and attitudes can be found in almost all doctors. They are a result of being human, being male, being capable of self-deception, and living and working within a subculture that subtly and powerfully supports the self-deception.

In this book I am talking about all doctors, and in the following stories you will see examples of a variety of ways in which patients can come to harm, at the hands of well-meaning physicians as well as with physicians who are simply bad people or bad doctors. Understanding what went wrong in each encounter will help you prevent such things from happening to you. Understanding how you can be led into unnecessary surgery by a doctor who thinks he is doing the right thing for you, and who you think is doing the right thing, is a key to grasping what is wrong with our system of health care and our typical doctor-patient relationship.

The first story is a good example, because it is about hysterectomy, an operation that is often done unnecessarily. About 20 million American women have had their uteruses removed, over half of those, I believe, unjustifiably. The reasons for the frequency of unnecessary hysterectomies range from doctors' purely mercenary behavior to their honest but erroneous belief that they are doing the right thing for their patients.

Many gynecologists feel that the uterus is a disposable organ, one that bleeds, cramps, carries babies, and gets cancer. These doctors seem to believe that it can be removed with no more effect than to make them heroes to their patients for having taken this miserable organ from them.

In fact, the uterus is a remarkable organ that performs amazing tasks during the lifetime of a woman. It is also a major anatomical structure, attached to, supporting, and being supported by many other structures. Its removal should not be taken lightly. Perhaps physicians have come to take it for granted because they feel its removal does not have the dire consequences produced by the removal of organs like kidneys, livers, parts of the intestine, or pieces of brain tissue.

Gynecologists should know better. They should be aware that no surgery can be performed without causing damage. They should know that removal of a uterus alters sexual experience for many women and causes great emotional distress for others. They should know, and take to heart, that any body part that does not absolutely have to be removed should be left alone. They should remember one of the basic tenets of medicine: *primum, non nocere,* "above all, do no harm."

But American gynecologists remove uteruses at about triple the rate of that in any country for which comparative statistics are available. Why? I wrote to the American College of Obstetrics and Gynecology, asking if the College had an official position on the question of whether women suffered abuse from gynecologists in such areas as unnecessary surgery. The Director of Practice Activities answered that "the College does not have an official position on the incidence of unnecessary surgery in the United States. A question frequently posed is what constitutes a correct rate for cesarean delivery, hysterectomy, and other procedures. There is, of course, no way to obtain data to answer such queries since rates for surgery as well as other medical procedures will vary widely among regions depending on availability of health care services and other factors."

He continued, "Although there is no way to set overall rates for surgery, there are methods to measure the appropriateness of individual procedures. The College, through its Department of Quality Assurance, produces criteria for evaluating a number of procedures according to widely accepted indications. These quality assurance tools are widely available to our Fellows and to hospitals."

In the final paragraph of his letter, he told me that current data showed a drop in the rate of hysterectomies and that new developments of alternative therapies might result in a further decline in the rate. He ended with, "This does not constitute a scientific response, but it would tend to argue against the charge of irresponsible overuse of gynecologic surgery by gynecologists." What he did not say is that ACOG is making a major effort to study whether or not there is a significant rate of unnecessary hysterectomy. He could not say this because there is no such study being conducted.

Such a study could be conducted, but it would require a decision on the part of the profession to determine the truth, and even then the truth would be hard to prove, because the facts about a given hysterectomy are not easily gleaned from the records as they exist. For example, the most common indication for hysterectomy listed on hospital records is fibroid tumors of the uterus. If you were to look closely at each case, you would find a large percentage of reports in which the fibroids, listed as though they were the reason for the operation, turned out to be an incidental finding. They may have been tiny and harmless, but were the only pathology found, so the final report looks like a justifiable hysterectomy done for fibroid tumors. This in spite of the fact that the fibroids were not found until surgery, or may only have been seen when the pathologist dissected the uterus, and nothing was found to support the preoperative diagnosis. The patient may have agreed to surgery in the belief that she had endometriosis or adenomyosis, or chronic pelvic inflammatory disease (PID), and may never have been told that nothing of the kind was found.

The second most commonly listed indication for hysterectomy is abnormal bleeding. If you looked closely at these records, you would find few cases where the bleeding was of such a severe nature as to have required the surgery, and where the surgery was a last resort after all else had failed. You would find many cases, however, where there was no tissue abnormality described by the pathologist that would justify a hysterectomy. Instead, you would probably find that the postoperative diagnosis (which is supposed to confirm the reason for the operation) says "metrorrhagia," irregular periods, or "menorrhagia," heavy periods. These conditions justify hysterectomy if other criteria are met, but the postoperative diagnosis and pathology report do not elaborate, so that having those words listed seems to imply that there was a valid indication for the operation. Statistics used to justify the large numbers of hysterectomies are very misleading.

Why, really, are hysterectomies done in excessive numbers? Not for any single reason. The reasons reflect all the factors in the world of women's health care that result in women being abused. Hysterectomies are deliberately sold to women by doctors who use the operation as their major source of income. They are done by well-meaning but misguided physicians who believe that women are better off without their uterus. They are done by doctors who respond to their patients' requests for a hysterectomy to end their periods and who are just unethical enough to tell themselves "if she wants it, why shouldn't I do it, and she obviously doesn't want to know about the risk." They are done by impatient doctors who don't want to spend the time it would take to try a succession of alternative therapies, or who are afraid that if they don't provide instant relief, the patient will go elsewhere. Mostly they are done by male physicians who were trained in a milieu that did nothing to alter their ingrained male prejudices about women and that reinforced the attitude that it is all right to decide for a woman what she needs, instead of giving her the knowledge and power to make the decision for herself. These doctors have felt no impetus to challenge the conventional wisdom of the gynecologic fraternity, and the shared misconceptions of the gynecologists' subculture have been passed through generations.

As with hysterectomies, the many other ways in which women are abused by their doctors result from a variety of factors. It is neither sufficient nor accurate to say that all, or most, gynecologists are simply bad people. The stories that follow illustrate some of the other factors. These are true stories about real patients and real doctors. I've given the doctors and the patients fictitious names for obvious reasons, but I have not altered the facts in any other way, nor have I exaggerated so as to make the stories more inflammatory. The kinds of things depicted by these patients' experiences occur every day, everywhere in the country, and are not unique situations that were difficult for me to find. I chose them from my experience in gynecology over a sixteen-year period and could cite many, many more. These represent some of the most common unfortunate actions, attitudes, and behaviors that women experience in their relationships with gynecologists.

I need to say here that this book is not about John Smith as a physician, and it is certainly not an attempt to portray myself as better than other doctors. I am sure that I have failed my patients many times in many ways, and if these stories seem to place me in some sort of infallible hero role, it was not my intention to create that impression. These patients happened to come to me already in trouble. Certainly many other doctors could have done whatever I did for them. I can only tell you true firsthand stories of situations that I personally experienced, and ask you to consider their significance as it might apply to you.

Six

THE MARKETING OF
AN OPERATION

IT IS IMPOSSIBLE FOR A GYNECOLOGIST TO PERFORM UNNECESSARY hysterectomies just to generate income unless the patients, for one reason or another, go along with the plan. Here is an illustration of how patients can be led into compliance by a trusted physician of long standing—how they think they've been given a realistic description of their condition and prognosis when, in fact, they have been misled. The example might suggest the difficulty of defending yourself against this kind of physician, but it should also serve to let you know that it doesn't have to happen to you if you are adequately prepared for each encounter with a doctor.

During my practice there was a gynecologist, with whom I sometimes consulted, who made the decision to retire. In spite of the fact that he announced this just three months before the retirement date, he scheduled and performed twenty-two hysterectomies in the month before he left. Since this was almost triple his usual month's production, I was astounded. Surely, he had not been ignoring that many of his patients who needed to have a hysterectomy in the previous months.

The explanation came weeks later, when a nurse who had worked for him told me about his private filing system. It seems he had kept a card file on all the patients to whom he had recommended a hysterectomy. When he decided to retire, he took it home and, at night, called them all. He told them that he was retiring and if they thought they would ever want to have a hysterectomy done, they should go ahead with it so that he could do it for them.

The amazing thing was not that he made the effort but that twenty-two women took him up on it! I looked at the records to try to understand, and what I found was essentially a lesson in salesmanship, on how to sell someone something they don't need.

With the limited number of good indications for doing a hysterectomy and the large number of possible complications from it, one would expect that few women would have this operation performed. In fact, it is done in staggering numbers, about 600,000 each year, and is easily one of the top three operations with regard to the frequency with which it is done unnecessarily. With a death rate of 1 out of 1,000, that means a toll of about 600 women each year dying from this operation. Why this number is so large, and grows each year, starts to become clear when you look at some significant numbers.

A vaginal hysterectomy takes from thirty to sixty minutes to perform and costs between $2,000 and $3,000, depending on where in the country you live. As with other medical procedures, the cost is not determined by supply and demand, but rather is controlled by physicians through a system that defies logic. If you look at a list of average charges for medical procedures and you know what each of them really involves, you see that the cost does not reflect any consistent, rational set of determining parameters.

There is no better example of this than hysterectomy. Given that most are done without a disease being present which requires that it be done, almost no skill is needed to make the decision to recommend it. The operation itself could be learned by almost anyone of reasonable intelligence. The charge for it does not vary with the length of time it takes to perform, or the difficulty of the particular case. It doesn't matter if the operation saved a life or made no difference at all; the charge is the same. Perhaps the charge should vary with the difficulty involved in selling the patient on having the operation, for that's often where the real skill lies.

In the case of the physician in this story, there was obviously a lot of sales skill present. Knowing him, however, I doubt that he ever consciously made up the sales approach. I'd think that it evolved over many years, and that once it had found an effective form it had remained consistent. I could trace a recurrent pattern in his records. After seeing a patient for routine visits for a while, he would make a note that said "menstrual cramps" or "deep-thrust dyspareunia" (this means that it hurts when your sex partner thrusts deeply during intercourse) or both. I should point out that neither of these things necessarily indicates any abnormality. At the next visit, he would note the same thing. After that, there would be two or three visits that ended with the note "still has cramps and deep-thrust dyspareunia, recommend hyst." Finally, there would be a note that said "still has symptoms, *wants* hyst" (emphasis added).

Speculating, on the basis of the records, I could guess that what he had done was this: He had first suggested to the patient that her experience of menstrual cramps and deep-thrust dyspareunia was abnormal. He then suggested that a hysterectomy would be a reasonable solution to her problem. And finally, after confidence had been established, he suggested to the patient that he thought it would be a good idea, in his professional judgment, for her to have the operation.

But "wants hyst" is not an acceptable diagnosis as an indication for hysterectomy, so the hospital record, subject to some scrutiny, unlike the office record, said other things. Most of the preoperative diagnoses would say something like "dysfunctional uterine bleeding" (irregular periods with no known cause), "metrorrhagia" (irregular periods of unspecified cause), "uterine prolapse" (the uterus has less support than it once did), or "dysmenor-rhea" (menstrual cramps).

None of these things can be verified by a pathologist when examining the removed uterus, or by a Professional Review Organization comparing preoperative diagnoses with the pathologist's findings. The admission history always used terms that suggested that the patient's life could not happily proceed without surgery, because of the severity of her menstrual cramps or her irregular periods.

Perhaps so, but were they really bad enough to take the risks of the operation? Why would a woman go through with it if not? The truth is that women generally are not given a clear picture of their real choices. The facts can be presented in many, many ways, and the way they are presented depends on whether the gynecologist wants the patient to have the operation, not to have the operation, or to make an informed and reasonable decision. Let me tell you some of the ways that women are led to the operating table.

Perhaps the most common technique is to suggest to a patient that hysterectomy is the only appropriate way to handle her problems, whatever they may be. Sometimes alternative treatments for things like menstrual cramps, menstrual pain, heavy periods, or irregular periods are not offered, or if they are, they are presented in a way that makes the patient think they have no good chance of working. At the same time, surgery is presented as though it has no significant risks and will cause little discomfort or inconvenience.

A physician can say to a patient, "I can take out your uterus and you will never have another period, never have to worry about birth control or cancer of the cervix or uterus, and all it means is perhaps five days in the hospital. Sure, there are complications sometimes, but significant ones are not common, and *my* patients rarely have problems." This sounds much easier to experience on a one-time basis than the prospect of a lifetime of cramps or bleeding problems.

But that physician could also say, "If we try everything and fail to resolve your problem, hysterectomy would be a last resort, but you should know that if you have a hysterectomy done you could die from a pulmonary embolus, you could hemorrhage after surgery and have to have a second operation to save your life, you could get a permanent passage of feces through your vagina, you could have a ureter inadvertently tied or cut and wind up losing a kidney, you could develop an infection that would require the subsequent removal of your ovaries, and you could conceivably end up with your vagina shortened so much that you may never experience comfortable intercourse again. In fact, some women report that orgasm never again feels the same after a hysterectomy; some report that they don't enjoy sex at all anymore. I think I'm a pretty good surgeon, but these complications happen to almost all surgeons sometime, and some bad effects can be expected even with uncomplicated surgery." That doesn't sound like the same operation being described, but in both examples no lies have been told.

It appears that this retiring doctor believed he was doing a good thing for his patients. It is also apparent to me that he convinced each of them that they needed the procedure without giving them the chance to really understand the possible consequences of "their" decision, and without helping them to understand their options. Another way to market the procedure is to create in the patient the perception that her options are limited. Here's a real example.

Many years ago, a new patient came into my office to get a second opinion about a hysterectomy. She had been seeing Dr. Houseman for a long time for routine checkups and on one occasion had complained of intermittent mild pain that seemed to occur about the same time in her menstrual cycle each month. She was told that she had "ovarian cysts" and was given a shot of Depo-Provera, the trade name of a long-acting form of the hormone progesterone.

Never mind that "ovarian cysts" is not a real diagnosis by itself, or that progesterone is not an appropriate treatment for her problem, or that, at the time, Depo-Provera had not been approved for clinical use. While Depo-Provera was being investigated as a possible once-a-month birth-control shot, studies had not proved whether the drug would increase the incidence of uterine, ovarian, or breast cancer in women. It also had as a side effect the production of irregular or continuous uterine bleeding. When this patient indeed developed persistent light bleeding, she called the doctor's office to tell him about it. The office nurse asked her to hold the phone while she reported this to Dr. Houseman. She came back to the phone and said, "Dr. Houseman said to ask you whether you wanted a D and C or a hysterectomy?" She decided she wanted another opinion, and that's when she called me.

When I explained that she really had nothing wrong with her that required treatment except for the effects of the Depo-Provera, she was quite relieved. She had not been bothered much by the mild discomfort she had described originally to Dr. Houseman, and only needed reassurance. After I got her bleeding straightened out, I followed her for years. She had no problems and passed into a comfortable menopause, after which she had no bleeding whatsoever to worry about.

Later, I saw a patient who said she sought my advice on behalf of five other women, all patients of Dr. Houseman's, and all of whom had been treated with Depo-Provera. All of them had also either developed irregular bleeding or had failed to have their symptoms resolve after the shot, and all had been offered a hysterectomy as a solution. It was hard not to believe that this was one of the ways Dr. Houseman kept his steady flow of an average five hysterectomies a week in the pipeline. He's still out there, as are many like him. If you encounter them forewarned and forearmed about the facts concerning hysterectomy and the sales techniques that might be used, you should wind up on the operating table only if you need and want to be there.

Keep in mind that health care is a business. Doctors would like to have you see them as thorough professionals, unsullied by such crass considerations as income and market share. Don't believe it! Not only are genuinely unethical and mercenary doctors actively marketing their operations, but well-intentioned doctors are doing it as well. In fact, the health-care system as a whole is actively pursuing you as a patient through the same techniques that everyone with a product is using to get you to be a customer. The danger lies in your failing to understand that. Be a smart and wary consumer, and keep the entire health-care system in the same perspective that you probably already have placed car dealers, insurance salesmen, and the makers of food products.

Seven

BETTER LEFT ALONE

BEING TOLD THAT THERE IS SOMETHING "ABNORMAL" IN HER BODY TENDS to make the average woman open to a suggestion that something should be done about it. Many unscrupulous doctors use that tendency to lead their patients into unnecessary surgery. The patient in the following story was almost a victim, and her case illustrates how so many hysterectomies are done with no other justification than the presence of harmless fibroid tumors.

Melody made an emergency appointment on a Friday afternoon. I was later to learn that she was an exceptionally bright, articulate, and poised young woman, but on that day she was so distraught that she could barely hold herself together.

At age thirty, engaged to a physician in another state, her life had been quite lovely until that morning, when she had seen a gynecologist for her first routine exam in several years. She was very athletic, knowledgeable about nutrition and fitness, and felt so healthy that she had no apprehensions about her exam. She probably wouldn't even have seen anyone except that she had begun taking birth-control pills a year earlier and wanted to get a checkup and refill before her wedding.

Following her exam, Dr. Crenshaw told her he had found a large mass in her pelvis, the nature of which he had not yet been able to diagnose. He sent her to the hospital X-ray department to have an ultrasound examination done. During ultrasound, sound waves are passed through the body and a picture is made of the pattern in which they bounce back to the machine. A useful tool in obstetrics, it lets us look at the developing fetus and monitor its growth. Ultrasound was not, at the time of this story, sufficiently sophisticated to be very useful in gynecology, since a skillful pelvic exam could still detect masses better. But even then it was occasionally helpful in determining whether a mass in the pelvis was solid or hollow, something that can be difficult to discern by pelvic exam alone.

After the ultrasound the doctor pulled no punches. The large mass appeared to be an ovarian tumor, he told her, and at her age it might well turn out to be cancer. He was having his nurse schedule her for surgery on Monday, and the surgery would almost certainly mean a hysterectomy, with removal of the tubes and ovaries as well. Any other discussion or explanation would just have to wait until after the surgery.

All of this was too much for Melody to absorb, or accept, so quickly. Frightened out of her wits, she called her fiancé in tears. Fortunately, he was not willing to have Melody rushed off to surgery without getting another opinion, especially when the whole picture made no sense—a large cancer in a young woman with no symptoms whatsoever? Very rare, indeed.

When I did my own exam, I had absolutely no doubt that I could give Melody some very good news, but wondered how I could make her share my certainty about the diagnosis.

There's an old adage told to every medical student early in the training process: "When you hear hoofbeats, don't think of zebras." This means that symptoms and abnormal findings should be interpreted as most likely representing something common, not as a disease that is seen once in a lifetime.

On my examination of Melody, I could easily feel not one,

but five round masses arising from the uterus. They were part of the uterus but clearly not ovarian tumors. Rather they seemed to be leiomyomata, fibroid tumors of the uterus, which are quite common and virtually always harmless. When I told her this, Melody burst into tears, sobbing, "How do I know who's right? He says I might die and you say I don't even need surgery." I tried to convince her that these things were so common, they had such a typical feel, and I could feel them so clearly that there simply wasn't any question. But I could tell she was unconvinced so I tried something different.

I drew a picture of exactly what I felt and told her exactly what I would recommend doing—discontinuing birth-control pills. I suggested that she allow each of my three partners to examine her, without talking to me or to one another, then have each of them draw their findings and make their recommendations. She agreed.

When they were all done, the four drawings were identical, the recommendations were identical, and each of the partners was so confident that Melody was convinced. Having four pelvic exams is not a pleasant experience, but Melody thought it was a pretty good swap for major surgery.

Together, we called her fiancé. Not only was he easily convinced, but he had talked to staff gynecologists at his teaching hospital and they had all said, "I bet she just has fibroids." Melody then called Dr. Crenshaw from my office to tell him to cancel her surgery. He was livid and tried to tell her she had to come by his office to sign a paper that relieved him of any responsibility if she were to die of cancer! Melody, rather than being frightened again by this nonsense, hung up on him.

Melody's uterus had produced these benign tumors under stimulation by the hormones in the birth-control pills. The pill doesn't cause fibroid tumors, but in women who are hereditarily prone to develop them the pill may make the tiny ones that already exist in the uterus grow rapidly. Except when they involve the inside lining of the uterus and cause severe and uncontrollable hemorrhaging with periods, or when they are so large that they put damaging pressure on other structures in the pelvis, they do not require hysterectomy or removal. If they cause discomfort or seem to be causing infertility, they can be removed from the uterus and everything else left intact. If left alone, they tend to shrink at menopause, when estrogen is no longer being produced and the uterine muscle fibers, which make up the tumors and which depend on estrogen, become smaller.

I followed Melody for eight years after her first office visit. The fibroids gradually became smaller and never caused any symptom. I never did have occasion to discuss with her what I thought would have happened if Dr. Crenshaw had opened her abdomen, but I would bet that he would have seen the fibroids, taken out her uterus, and told her that it was just as well, since he was in there anyway. Would that have harmed her, changed her sexually, changed her physically? The answer is yes, absolutely, and since she is a healthy and happy woman today, it is obvious that she could have only been made worse by surgery. In addition, this woman would have lost the option of future pregnancy.

It is important to understand that much of the gynecological surgery done today produces absolutely no benefit for the patient, and that there is no such thing as surgery without harmful effect.

Fibroid tumors are the most common diagnostic indication for hysterectomies in America, even though their presence alone calls for no treatment at all. Many ovarian cysts fall in the same category of a harmless condition that is used as an excuse for surgery. Endometrial polyps, cervical dysplasia, and irregular periods are others. It is too easy for a doctor to tell you you have something "abnormal" and convince you that you would somehow be better off if it was removed, especially if the doctor fails to tell you, in true detail, what that removal may do to you.

Any intrusion into your abdomen or pelvic cavity will cause harm. Even simply opening the abdomen, touching its contents, and closing it again will result in adhesions, and those adhesions can lead to infertility, pain, bowel obstruction, painful intercourse, painful bowel movements, or painful urination. If something is actually cut, traumatized, or removed, the likelihood of these complications increases, and consequences related to the specific organs involved will also occur. When it comes to your body, in the absence of a compelling reason to do otherwise, it is better left alone.

Eight

MORE THAN A UTERUS AT STAKE

IT MAY SURPRISE YOU TO LEARN THAT DOCTORS CAN MISS DIAGNOSES AND jeopardize their patients' lives for reasons other than incompetence or negligence. Here is a case in which a doctor was unable to evaluate what he was seeing and hearing because of his prejudices about the emotional makeup of women and because of his own inability to see clearly anything that threatened his self-image. There was significant incompetence involved as well, but the character of the man was the major factor.

Judy's appointment with me was scheduled for 1:30 p.m., the first one of the afternoon. Sitting in the waiting room alone at 12:45, she looked so obviously distressed that my office nurse brought her back to an exam room early and let me know she was there. I was glad for the extra time because she had a lot to tell me, and a great need to talk to someone.

"I want you to know that if you think I'm crazy too, I'm ready to see a psychiatrist now" were her first words. "I've almost lost my husband and my job, and I think I'm losing my mind."

Three months ago Judy had had a hysterectomy, performed by Dr. Palmer, a gynecologist whom she had known for quite some time. The reason for the surgery was somewhat unclear to her, but she had such positive feelings about this charming gynecologist that she had not questioned his recommendation. Apparently, she had experienced some irregular bleeding and menstrual cramps, and he had expressed the opinion that she "would be better off with it out," referring to her uterus. The procedure had gone smoothly, as far as she knew, but postoperatively she had run a low-grade fever, with alarming spikes to very high levels. Spiking fevers are never a normal postoperative event. She had also had pain, which began on the fourth day post-op and which seemed to her to be different from the initial postsurgical pain. Dr. Palmer had told her she "probably had a little infection at the top of the vagina," placed her on an oral antibiotic, and sent her home from the hospital.

At home, her pain waxed and waned and she felt intermittently feverish, symptoms which she reported to her doctor by phone. He reassured her repeatedly that she was having a normal array of posthysterectomy symptoms and, during the third call, suggested that she was being a "bit hysterical." He then requested that she hold any further reports until he saw her in the office at four weeks.

She was determined to stick it out, and made it to her appointment in spite of the continuation of the symptoms and the development of an annoying vaginal discharge, which had a bad odor. After waiting for an hour in the waiting room, she had prepared a mental list of the things she wanted to tell the doctor, but he made it clear that he didn't have the time to listen.

Rushing through an uncomfortable exam, he chatted reassuringly about how normal everything seemed to be, except for a small amount of "granulation tissue" at the top of the vagina, where the sutures had been, and above which all the cut and ligated blood vessels, connective tissue, and the tubes and ovaries were gathered after the uterus was removed. This he cauterized with silver nitrate, without warning her. The resulting pain left her trembling, pale, and nauseated while he rushed out, telling her to come back for a final check in two more weeks.

Back at home, she at first felt angry, then ashamed that she had been so whiny. Surely, Dr. Palmer knew what she was experiencing and was able to tell if something was wrong, or if everything was going normally. She vowed again to tough it out until all this was over. For the first time she wondered if the surgery had been worth it. At least she'd have no more menstrual periods, and no more worries about birth control, but if she had known beforehand what it would be like, would she have gone through with it?

That night her husband, who had been very tolerant of her incapacity, wondered if the doctor had said it was all right for them to have intercourse yet. She told him that he hadn't mentioned it, but she was still having pain, and thought it was a bad idea. He also shyly asked if the doctor had told her how long the odor was going to last. She was stunned by this because she had not realized it was noticeable to him. After he was asleep, she took the first of many long, hot baths, feeling less attractive and less self-confident than she could ever remember.

Two weeks later, she returned for her six weeks' check, still experiencing a painful sensation of pressure in her lower abdomen, and still having an intermittent discharge from her vagina. She didn't like being examined when she felt so unclean, but she knew that it had to be done if the doctor was to help her. He finished quickly and returned after she had dressed to tell her everything seemed just fine. Judy protested mildly that she didn't feel fine, and that she didn't understand why she still had the discharge and odor. "Probably a yeast infection," he said, "from the antibiotics after surgery. I'll give you some cream to use, and you'll be good as new. I don't need to see you again, so you should see someone in about a year for a routine physical. Good luck."

Judy describes feeling at that time as if she had been cast adrift, and she turned to her husband for support. She didn't know what was wrong, but she knew that she still felt awful, with the discharge continuing in spite of the vaginal cream and the pain seeming to worsen now and then. In addition, she felt totally devoid of energy, and she cried often, seemingly without cause. Her husband tried to listen and to be sympathetic, but he knew the doctor had told her she was well, and the doctor certainly should know. Judy had not been herself since the operation, and he was more than ready to have his wife back. Was it her hormones?

Over the next month a pattern of symptoms began to emerge. Judy, still tired and weak, would develop increasing pelvic pain and pressure, then would have a gush of fluid from her vagina. This was more watery and more profuse than the discharge she had experienced up to then. The first time it happened she had rushed in to see her doctor, frightened but feeling that "now he would find out what was wrong." After his exam, Dr. Palmer seemed uncomfortable, and told her that he couldn't find anything abnormal. The fluid? Well, there was none there now, so just go home and try to relax.

It didn't go away. In spite of a growing feeling of uncleanliness and a physical lack of well-being, Judy tried to cope with the demands of her world. At work, she had trouble concentrating, being obsessed with thoughts about her condition, and found herself exhausted when the day was half through. Her boss, who had been understanding while she took her medical leave, was visibly reaching the limits of his sympathy. He called her in to say that he was as understanding as anyone about women's medical problems, but after nine weeks she should be back to normal. He told her to go home and not to come back until she had seen her doctor and gotten everything straightened out. Her husband didn't take the news well. He had grown increasingly silent when Judy had failed to snap out of it, and their disastrous attempts at sex had left him turning his attention to the T.V. set, or anything else that would take his mind off of his wife and her problems. Now her job was in jeopardy, and they needed the income. He demanded that she see her gynecologist, and maybe get referred to someone who could help her, perhaps a psychologist, or their minister.

This time the doctor was clearly annoyed. He didn't have time for an exam and just gave her another prescription for a different vaginal cream, "in case there's some kind of infection there that I missed." Again she went home and back to work, vowing that she would be well.

But the symptoms continued. Sometimes the gushes of fluid would happen at work, and sometimes she would wake up with the bed wet. Her husband withdrew from her, and once again, now three months after the operation, she turned in desperation to Dr. Palmer.

At this visit he did an exam, since she insisted that on that very morning she had awakened with the bed wet. Each time that happened, she said, her pain and pressure would lessen for a while.

He found nothing, but this time he didn't bother to patronize or to get her out of the office with some temporizing medication. He angrily told Judy that in his opinion there was nothing physically wrong with her, and unless she wanted him to refer her to a psychiatrist, he never wanted to see her again.

Devastated, she turned to her husband, who expressed his own lack of understanding about all of her problems and suggested that perhaps the doctor was right after all. Her closest friend was more helpful. A patient of mine, she suggested that Judy see me for another opinion, which was how she arrived at my office in a state of total self-doubt and emotional and physical exhaustion.

My examination helped, but did not answer all the questions. Upon a careful look at the top of Judy's vagina, with the aid of a magnifying instrument, I found a very small opening, into which I could pass a small probe. There should be no opening at the top of the vagina after healing from a hysterectomy. The top of the vagina is left closed and smooth, no longer with the cervix at the top. The upper end of the vagina, because it is sutured closed at the end of a hysterectomy, is referred to as the "cuff." I could feel no abnormal mass (lump) above the vaginal cuff, even though the exam was very painful for her (which is totally abnormal three months after a hysterectomy).

I told Judy that I had no doubt that there was a very real cause for her symptoms, and that together we would determine the cause and fix it. Even though I did not yet have the diagnosis, I knew that there were only two valid possibilities, given the clinical picture and knowing the anatomy involved and the limited number of things that could go wrong during or after hysterectomy. Something had to be affixed to the top of the vagina, inside the pelvis, that could collect fluid and intermittently eject it through an abnormal connection to the vagina. The only two structures that could be involved, either through a postoperative infection, a surgical error, or both, would be the ovary or the fallopian tube.

As I explained to Judy, one of the known possible complications of hysterectomy is prolapse of the fallopian tube. In the course of removing the uterus, the tube must be cut free from its attachment to the uterus, and the cut end tied shut and attached to the side of the pelvis. This leaves the rest of the tube, including its fimbriated end (the end with fimbriae, fingerlike projections, which normally pick up the egg and transport it into the uterus after fertilization) hanging suspended in the pelvic cavity in essentially normal position. As the top of the vagina and the peritoneum (the lining of the abdominal and pelvic cavities) are sewed closed, this free end can prolapse (fall into) the open area, and accidentally be trapped in the line of sutures, leaving the fimbriated end of the tube sewn into the top of the vagina, and the tube thus closed at both ends.

The ovary is closely associated with the tube and is therefore also left very close to the top of the vagina after hysterectomy. If there is infection postoperatively at the top of the vaginal-cuff closure (which is not uncommon), the ovary may become infected itself and adhere to the vagina, causing one of various clinical pictures, all of which are quite serious and potentially fatal.

After I described these two possibilities to Judy, her response was more relief than fear. She was ready to do, or have done, anything to restore her life to normalcy. We scheduled surgery, to consist of a laparoscopy first, to be sure that there was nothing inside that would require a different specialist or a different preparation for surgery. Laparoscopy is a procedure where a small incision is made in the bottom of the belly button and a slender instrument is passed into the abdomen, through which one can look into the pelvis. It is used both for diagnosis and for doing small operations such as tubal ligation, without actually opening the abdomen. In this case, I planned to go ahead with a larger lower-abdominal incision if I saw what I expected to see. Actually, as I told Judy, if I could have then felt a mass above the vagina, I would have been certain enough of the diagnosis to proceed directly with the bigger incision.

I obtained the records from Judy's hospitalization for her hysterectomy, and got little help. Although the temperature chart clearly showed an abnormal pattern of fever beginning on post-op day four, the physician's progress notes said only "doing well," and didn't even list that much every day, some days having no notation at all. Judy was discharged in spite of continuing fever—a terrible mistake, as the fever was definitely abnormal and no explanation for it had been sought. Any of the possible causes of such a post-op fever would be serious, and some of them life-threatening.

In the operating room, before going to sleep, Judy was smiling and happy: evidently, an impending general anesthetic and major surgery seemed a pleasant relief compared to her recent life experience. She told me that during the previous night she had felt the severe pain and pressure that had always preceded the expulsion of fluid from her vagina. Because of this, as soon as she was under the anesthetic I did a pelvic exam prior to anything else. What I felt was astonishing! There was a fluid-filled mass, easily eight inches in diameter, fixed to the vaginal apex inside the pelvis. I bypassed the laparoscopy and proceeded with a lower-abdominal incision. Inside, I found a gigantic left ovary, filled with purulent fluid and fixed to the top of the vagina. The small opening in the vagina I had seen in the office passed into this ovary. There had apparently been a postoperative ovarian abscess that had stuck to the vaginal cuff, drained through the vagina, and then proceeded to gradually fill with fluid. When the pressure was great enough, it would eject the fluid through the vagina. After this it would be like an empty balloon, and thus impossible to feel.

The fallopian tube was stretched thinly over the ovary, and when both were removed, the pelvic organs that remained, including her other tube and ovary, were normal. In the surgical lounge I was a little shell-shocked. This woman had lived for over three months with a postoperative complication that is often fatal! And though it appeared in a very unusual way and the patient had obviously tolerated her pain better than most of us would have, it made me angry to remember how she had been treated by the physician that had created the problem in the first place. He had actually told her to leave his office and never come back, that her symptoms weren't real, and that she needed a psychiatrist!

Fortunately, Judy had no post-op complications this time, and when I saw her for the final visit some six months after the operation, the change in her was remarkable. She looked great, having lost twenty pounds and progressed well into an aerobics program. She positively sparkled with enthusiasm for life, and she told me that the whole experience, though it had put her at the rock bottom, had made her start anew with her marriage, her job, her body, and her self-concept. She told me that she had thought seriously of filing a malpractice suit against the physician who had brought all this about, but now preferred to let it drop, so that she wouldn't carry the anger and bad memories into her new life. I had mixed feelings. Though Judy's well-being was obviously far more important than anything else, I knew too much about this particular physician, and knew that Judy was not the first, and would not be the last, to be harmed by him.

How did I know? In fact, after practicing in any given area for a short time, a physician knows who the good doctors are, who the charlatans are, who's crazy, who's taking drugs, and, most easily, who does a lot of surgery with minimal or no indication. This doctor I had also learned about most directly.

One afternoon a nurse who had previously been my patient, but whom I had not seen for two years, showed up on my schedule. I was glad to see her, as I remembered her as a delightful person, but I was curious to learn why she had been away so long. She seemed embarrassed as she explained that she had gotten a job as the office nurse for Dr. Palmer. Then she blurted out, "Can I please talk to you? I have to talk to someone about it. I quit that job because I couldn't stand to watch it anymore, someone has to stop the man."

She proceeded to tell me that in the beginning she liked this physician a lot. He seemed utterly charming with his patients, even though he kept himself terribly busy and spent little time with them. After a while she realized that he did more surgery than anyone she had ever seen, and that even though she did the scheduling, most of the time she didn't usually understand why the operation was being done. She came to feel that he simply charmed his patients until they trusted him completely, then recommended a hysterectomy.

The last straw came one day when he saw a patient who

wanted to have her tubal ligation reversed, a microsurgical procedure that takes a great deal of special training and practice. Microsurgical procedures are done under a microscope, using tiny sutures
and specialized instruments. These procedures were developed to
perform surgical tasks on such a small and delicate scale that it is
even hard to watch with the naked eye.

Knowing that, at that time, there was only one gynecologist in
town who had the proper training and experience in this kind of
surgery, she wondered if Dr. Palmer would refer the patient to that
physician. Instead, he came out of the exam room and told her to
schedule the procedure for himself. She pointed out that he had
never done such a procedure, and he replied that anyone could do it
and that he would read about it before trying it. But after four
hours in the operating room, he abandoned the effort and told the
patient that it just couldn't be done. The patient subsequently went
to an experienced physician in another town, had the procedure
done, and became pregnant. Fortunately, the tubes had not been
damaged beyond repair by Dr. Palmer's clumsy attempt.

It was true, Dr. Palmer had one of the busier surgical schedules in his town. Assuming that even an average number of his
hysterectomies were unnecessary, how could he get away with it?
Most people assume that someone watches over the activities of
physicians. In fact, the federal government requires that studies,
called audits, be done in every hospital that receives federal funds. I
remember well an audit done in Dr. Palmer's hospital. It was a
typical example of the lack of value in this method of monitoring
physicians. This study was a review of records concerning hysterectomy, and the criteria evaluated concerned issues that had no chance
of determining whether the operation was indicated or whether an
abnormal rate of complications occurred. It consisted of a checklist
that asked if there was a history and physical on the chart, if there

was a diagnosis in the history and physical, if the diagnosis was consistent with the pathology report, and if the patient had had a pre-op Pap smear. A letter from the audit committee to all the gynecologists reported the results, concluding, "We can congratulate ourselves, it is obvious that unnecessary hysterectomies are not being done in our hospital"!

Such self-deception is common among physicians. I'm sure that Dr. Palmer tells himself that he has few complications resulting from his medical care—though that would appear to be less than accurate.

Judy was a perfect example of how much is at stake when a hysterectomy is done. Her surgery deprived her of so much more than the absence of her uterus. It ultimately damaged her self-image, her sense of well-being, and her sexuality and threatened her marriage, her job, and her life!

When I wrote to Dr. Palmer, with Judy's permission, and told him of my findings at surgery, I expected a response of some kind, but neither I nor Judy ever heard from him. I have had occasion to learn of other cases in which this doctor has caused harm, and in all of them he has made it clear by his statements and actions that he was certain he had done nothing improper. His egotism is insurmountable. He is charming and convincing to his patients because he genuinely believes that he can do no harm. He also believes that surgery can make all his patients happier and healthier. I haven't encountered many doctors with his seemingly limitless capacity for self-deception, but doctors like him are the most dangerous. Be aware that they exist, and don't be reassured by charm and a slick, self-assured presentation. Look through all that to the facts, ask the essential questions, and decide what you need and want. Be a buyer; don't be sold.

Nine

AN EQUAL-OPPORTUNITY DISEASE

BLACK AND FEMALE, LESLIE WAS PROBABLY ACCUSTOMED TO PREJUDICE IN her life. I'd be willing to bet, though, that this time she had experienced a kind of prejudicial treatment that she didn't know existed.

She was twenty-six, married, well-educated, and was unable to get pregnant. A month before I met her, she had seen Dr. Siemens, a board-certified ob-gyn specialist, who she hoped could help her. She described for him all of her symptoms. These included painful periods, pain with intercourse, and, just before her period each month, severe abdominal swelling. She had also noticed that her bowel movements were painful, but only on the days just prior to her period. Even though she had used no birth control since her marriage two years before, she had been unable to conceive.

After he examined her, Dr. Siemens told Leslie that she apparently had a few fibroids of the uterus, and that she had chronic pelvic inflammatory disease with scarring and adhesions inside. He suggested that she get rid of her pain, and her chances of ever getting pregnant, by letting him do a hysterectomy and removing her tubes and ovaries. He seemed so sure of what he was saying that she almost let him schedule surgery. But she decided to think about it and to talk it over with her husband, who insisted that she get another opinion.

As I listened to her symptoms and asked a few questions, I

was already thinking that Leslie was giving me a perfect description of endometriosis. It didn't make sense that she would be a candidate for chronic pelvic inflammatory disease, as she had never used an IUD, had no history of venereal infection, and had experienced sex only with her husband, both before and after marriage. She was surprised to learn that what Dr. Siemens had diagnosed could only have developed from a previous venereal disease. He had simply failed to mention it.

When I did a pelvic exam there was no doubt. In addition to the many fibroid tumors on her uterus, Leslie had findings that could only be one of two things—cancer or endometriosis. At age twenty-six, cancer was not impossible, but nearly so. That made the diagnosis of endometriosis veritably certain. Nothing else feels like it, and it is so common that any other tentative diagnosis was way out in left field.

Why did Dr. Siemens make an off-the-wall diagnosis like chronic pelvic inflammatory disease when he should have thought of endometriosis first? The answer, I'm afraid, is that Leslie was black. For a long time, in textbooks and in residency training, gynecologists have been told that endometriosis isn't found in black women. I don't know how that particular myth got started. Maybe the statistics were skewed because many years ago black women didn't have as much access to medical care, or because they were less likely to be able to afford infertility investigation. More likely, it is because gynecologists also stereotype black women as being quite fertile, feeling that they have too many children, and thus don't think of them as candidates for a disease that causes infertility.

At any rate, it is quite clear now that endometriosis occurs in black women as frequently as in women of any other racial or ethnic background. Old gynecologic textbooks describe a "typical endometriosis patient" as white and slim, a career woman who has never been pregnant and is "emotionally high strung." In the past, if a woman was black, a housewife, or a mother, and especially if she was a calm and stoic version of any of those, she simply would not be evaluated for endometriosis. None of these stereotypes are accurate predictors of endometriosis, by the way: Dr. Siemens made a diagnosis based on racial prejudice.

But just as racial bias is not uncommon, many other types of prejudice also come into play in the gynecologist's office, not the least of which are the basic prejudices that women are less competent and rational than men and that women are promiscuous if they exercise the same freedom as men to enjoy and explore their sexuality. It's amazingly hard to get rid of the prejudices learned from significant people in our lives, such as parents or mentors. As a medical student, I heard so often that women who got gallstones were "fat, forty, with four kids" (a mnemonic device often heard in teaching hospitals) that it took forever for me to see slender unmarried women as candidates for gallbladder disease.

Some of the more commonly observable prejudices among physicians don't have the excuse of having been learned in medical school, and they are as petty and mean as you will see in any segment of our society. For instance, many gynecologists are totally unable to consider obese women as sexual beings. Many are completely unable to relate to a patient compassionately if she discloses that she is a lesbian (this usually comes up when a patient is asked what she uses for birth control; most gynecologists automatically assume heterosexuality). Patients who admit to having had numerous sex partners are perceived as not worthy of a great deal of time or effort and as "deserving what they get" if they contract a sexually transmitted disease.

Oftentimes, it seems, the only thing that elevates a male gynecologist to a level of appropriate respect for women is that he has an intelligent, competent wife who insists on being something more than his shadow and helps him to see women through less biased eyes. My own wife has helped me grow from the belief that I was completely sensitive, caring, and understanding about the needs of women to the knowledge that I had never genuinely been able to put myself in the position of the women whom I cared for. It wasn't easy, but I know that changes of perspective are possible. For men, healthy relationships with good women are essential for learning, and for gynecologists that means healthy relationships with their patients as well.

If Dr. Siemens had proceeded with his plan for Leslie, he undoubtedly would have opened her abdomen and removed her uterus, tubes, and ovaries, committing her to menopause at age twenty-six and leaving her hopeless sterility. By knowing what her exact status was, through laparoscopy, and by *valuing her desires,* I was able to bring about a better outcome.

I opened Leslie's abdomen and, using the laser, vaporized all the areas of endometriosis and all the adhesions and removed all the fibroid tumors from her uterus. Her symptoms were completely alleviated; a year later she became pregnant and in time delivered a healthy infant.

As I've discussed in previous chapters, prejudices about women dramatically affect diagnosis and treatment in women's medical care. This is especially true in the areas where typical male prejudices and lack of understanding about women are most prominent, and where other stereotyping is most common. These areas include race, sexual preference, sexual practices, and emotionality, as well as female assertiveness and every other kind of prejudice to which men subject women.

Leslie probably would not have quickly believed my diagnosis over that of Dr. Siemens had she not learned that his diagnosis depended on her having contracted a venereal disease at a time in her life when that was not possible. But every woman should know that her doctor may, on any occasion, make a diagnosis that is influenced by the fact that she is black, or a lesbian, or has a history of venereal disease—or that she may not be taken seriously simply because she is a woman.

Ten

A SMALL MISTAKE

DOCTORS MAKE MISTAKES. THEY WOULD LIKE TO PRETEND THAT THEIR mistakes never happened. I have known many cases in which a mistake in the operating room was never admitted to the patient. I have known cases where a doctor made a mistake in the operating room and never admitted it to himself. This is a case that could have been both.

The treatment of infertility is often unsuccessful. If the patient loses hope under her initial treatment, many times she'll choose to try a new doctor. Lisa was such a patient, and her history was not unusual, or so it seemed.

At age twenty-eight, after trying to become pregnant for nine months, she had sought the help of Dr. Carson, who was not an infertility specialist but was a board-certified ob-gyn specialist. After he had performed a laparoscopy, he told her that she had endometriosis, which is the cause of infertility in about one-third of all cases. He recommended surgery, to consist of an incision into her abdomen followed by three procedures: first, the removal of the areas of endometriosis; second, an operation called a presacral neurectomy; and, finally, a particular type of uterine suspension (an operation that fixes the uterus in a forward-tilting position). All of this he had done two years before I saw her. When she told me this I was a little surprised, because even at that time a great deal of new knowledge gained from developments in microsurgery and infertility had cast two of those procedures into disfavor.

In the presacral neurectomy, the nerves that carry pain messages from the uterus are cut. The procedure was first developed years ago as a treatment for severe menstrual cramps; because many women with endometriosis also have menstrual pain, its use was widened to include those women as well. Some people believed, and still do, that the operation also had some unknown beneficial effect on endometriosis.

Research in infertility surgery, however, had made it clear that *any* surgery in the pelvis should be avoided if at all possible. This is because the adhesions that result from the procedure can impair fertility. For this reason, too, the various operations to suspend the uterus had been abandoned entirely.

In suspension procedures, the uterus is sewn to other structures in such a way as to hold it both forward and higher in the pelvic cavity. This procedure had been developed because of the mistaken notion that a "tilted" uterus had something to do with infertility. When it became clear, a long time ago, that this was not the case and that the operation could *cause* infertility, it was no longer recommended.

I wondered if there was something unusual about Lisa's case that had caused Dr. Carson to approach it this way, so I sent for his records before doing anything else. There weren't any real surprises, except that while he described almost no endometriosis in his operative note, he had proceeded anyway to do both the presacral neurectomy and the uterine suspension.

The type of suspension he performed is called a "Gilliam" suspension, and he described it in his operative summary as having been done in routine fashion. Perhaps I should describe what a "routine" Gilliam suspension is supposed to be.

Two thick, ropelike ligaments, called the "round ligaments," run from the top of the uterus, on each side, to the side of the inner surface of the pelvic cavity. From there, they travel through the inguinal canal into the labia. In a Gilliam suspension, these ligaments are pulled through an incision made in a layer of the front wall of the abdomen and are sewn there with permanent silk suture. This holds the uterus up and forward.

After doing this surgery, Dr. Carson had followed Lisa for almost two years, without her getting pregnant. He had treated her with fertility drugs over many cycles, even though he had never made a diagnosis which indicated that she might benefit from them. Discouraged with the lack of success, Lisa decided to try someone else.

Because Dr. Carson had made a diagnosis of endometriosis, and because he had done extensive surgery, I decided to do a laparoscopy to determine if Lisa had recurrent endometriosis. I also wanted to see if her previous surgery had resulted in adhesions involving her tubes and ovaries, as this can result from any pelvic operation. What I found was quite amazing!

Looking in through the laparoscope, I needed a while to be sure of what I was seeing: Lisa's fallopian tubes had been pulled through the fascial layer of the abdomen and sewn there, effectively blocking them completely. Instead of pulling the round ligaments through, Dr. Carson had mistakenly grabbed the fallopian tubes. He had, in effect, done a tubal ligation, a sterilization procedure, on an infertility patient!

In the recovery room, Lisa and her husband were furious. After venting a lot of anger, Lisa began to recount all the treatments —eighteen months of keeping daily temperature charts and timing intercourse, so that sex had become more of a job than a pleasure— and then she remembered the pain of the surgery.

"But why didn't he see that the tubes were blocked when he did that X ray?"

"What X ray?" I said.

"After the surgery, while I was still in the hospital, Dr. Carson sent me down to X ray and did one of those tests where you put dye through the tubes."

"I didn't know about that. What did he tell you about it?"

"He never mentioned it, so I assumed it was normal."

I knew it wasn't possible for that X ray to have shown her tubes to be normal. I sent for the X-ray report from the hospital. It read "Dye does not pass through the tubes, but according to the clinical history, the tubes were open at surgery."

Why had he ordered the test in the first place, and why did he do nothing about the findings? Had he lied? Had he known that he had closed her tubes and pretended not to know, while he treated her for nonexistent problems? I still don't know the answers to those questions for sure, but I have strong suspicions.

Lisa still desperately wanted to get pregnant, and it would be impossible with her tubes as they were, so a few weeks later we went back to the operating room. In a three-hour microsurgical procedure I was able to successfully free the tubes from the abdominal wall, remove the scarred midportion, and reanastomose (put back together) the two ends. This time, a follow-up X ray showed that they were open.

At the request of Lisa's attorney I had videotaped the surgery, a microsurgical procedure. A camera mounted on the microscope produced a good-quality documentation of what had been done previously, as well as what was done this time. It was an unusual thing to do, but there was clearly going to be a malpractice suit, and I thought the incontrovertible documentation would produce an out-of-court settlement, thus reducing the trauma for Lisa, and even for Dr. Carson, though I admit that the latter was not a high priority for me.

Sure enough, a suit was filed; unfortunately, Lisa had to go through hours of legal deposition, as did her husband, myself, and Dr. Carson. I was curious to know what he would give as an explanation, and I hoped that he would just say he had made a surgical error and accept the consequences.

In his deposition he described the technique of the suspension in detail, especially the part of the procedure where he blindly passes a clamp through a hole in the fascia and asks his assistant to place the round ligaments in the clamp. His assistant, he said, was an inexperienced family practitioner, and had placed the *tubes* in the clamp instead. It was not his own fault, and the assistant should be the one being sued. As far as I know, Lisa and her husband are still together and the case was settled out of court, but I understand that Dr. Carson's assistant doesn't operate with him, or speak to him, anymore. I have lost touch with Lisa, and do not know if she has succeeded in becoming pregnant.

Virtually no one knows about that case, or the lawsuit, or the outcome. If malpractice suits have any value it is not in taking money from the insurance carrier and giving it to a patient who has been damaged. The patients aren't made whole again by money. The value is that bad physicians are subject to some kind of accountability, and the fact that they are bad physicians can be made public. In actual practice, it doesn't work that way. The very worst cases of physician negligence or incompetence, which result in malpractice suits, are settled out of court because the attorneys know they are indefensible. As a result, no one ever hears about them.

Unfortunately, malpractice suits filed by avaricious lawyers or misguided patients against good physicians who did the best job anyone could have done but got a bad result *do* go to court, and thus to the newspapers. In those cases, frequently an excellent physician is maligned publicly, and wrongly.

It's a bad system, but it is the only part of the health-care system that gives patients a chance to open all their records to scrutiny and professional review. With bad doctors, it may also be the only way patients ever learn the truth about what was done to them, especially with operations done through instruments like laparoscopes, colonoscopes, or arthroscopes, or those done under a microscope. In those procedures, the only person who can see what is going on is the operating surgeon.

Many things about the way malpractice litigation is handled need to be changed, and I will address that in the Epilogue. But, meanwhile, it is important to know that doctors don't always own up to their errors. As I've said before, doctors are just like other people, and many people are easily prone to employing situational ethics ("I know this is usually wrong, but in this case I think it's the only thing to do"). How many people, if asked to admit to a mistake from their past that couldn't be proved, would deny it (and maybe convince themselves it never happened)? Doctors do these things often. If you add the malpractice threat to common human behavior, it should not be surprising that your doctor's mistakes may not be divulged to you. If you are suspicious for any reason, get some outside help, get the records, and investigate. It may be the only way you'll get the truth.

Eleven

CONSPIRACY OF THE BROTHERHOOD

THERE IS A PERVASIVE FEELING OF FRATERNITY AMONG PHYSICIANS, especially strong among gynecologists, and it can result in a conflict of interest between a patient's welfare and the protection of the other fellows. In this story, the bond extended beyond the doctors themselves to include drug companies, insurance companies, and attorneys. And it was not a single patient who was harmed, but thousands.

Jan was a patient who became very special to me, perhaps because I worked so hard, and for so long a time, to help her, and failed totally.

She first came to see me as an infertility patient, having tried unsuccessfully for two years to become pregnant. Many times the initial history from a patient or the physical exam will lead you close to the cause of infertility; obvious genetic disorders, total absence of normal menstrual cycles, a husband who has no sperm or who is an alcoholic, congenital abnormalities of the reproductive system, a history of serious pelvic infection or a ruptured appendix, previous surgery on the tubes or ovaries, or obvious symptoms or findings of endometriosis—these things will at least suggest to an infertility specialist where to place emphasis in the evaluation. Jan had none of these. In other words, there was no hint of a possible cause of her inability to become pregnant.

She was twenty-eight, married for six years, and had normal periods, a normal medical history, usual sexual practices, and a completely normal physical exam. After the history and physical, the first step in the evaluation of infertility is to determine whether the problem resides in the husband or the wife or both. Jan's husband had a normal semen analysis and a normal history and physical. In males, these two things almost completely rule out the possibility of his being the source of the trouble.

Jan had never had a serious illness; had had almost no sexual experience prior to marriage, except with her husband; and had never been pregnant. She had avoided pregnancy by having had a Copper-7 intrauterine device (IUD) inserted at the time of her marriage, which she had retained for three years before having it removed. She had used foam for contraception for a year, then began trying to conceive.

After trying all the simple and routine tests for infertility, I proceeded to do an X-ray procedure (called a hysterosalpingogram) in which a dye is squirted into the cavity of the uterus through the cervix. If the tubes are normal, the dye will enter the tubes, pass through them, and fall freely into the pelvic cavity. Because the dye shows up on an X ray, the test can be watched on a monitor screen.

In Jan's case, the dye filled the cavity of the uterus but would not even enter the tubes. This told me that something was wrong, but not exactly what, or how bad, it was. The next step, then, was to do a laparoscopy so that I could look inside the abdomen and view the uterus, tubes, and ovaries. At the same time I could attach a device to the cervix that would enable me to squirt a blue dye through the cervix and uterus while I was looking inside. Laparoscopy has become an invaluable tool in the investigation of infertility, especially in the circumstances that turned out to be Jan's problem. It involves a small incision in the bottom of the belly button through which a slender instrument like a telescope is passed. With it you can get a clear look inside the abdomen, and by using other instruments, which are passed through separate one-eighth-inch incisions, some types of surgery can also be done.

When I looked inside I found the typical picture of someone who has had a previous, devastating infection involving the tubes and ovaries. The tubes themselves were adhered to surrounding structures, they were completely closed at their ends, and they were slightly swollen, as though they had fluid in them. The dye that I instilled into the uterus did not enter the tubes at all, much less pass through and spill freely out the ends. All of this is often the aftermath of severe gonorrhea infections or infections of other kinds, or it can result from pelvic surgery of any kind. Jan had no history of any of these things. It should have been a surprise and a total shock to me, but it wasn't, for in my practice I saw probably fifty women with the same picture from the same cause—the IUD!

The IUD, or intrauterine device, is a contraceptive device with a long history. It is said that this type of birth control has been used for thousands of years, perhaps the first example having been in the Middle East, where camel drivers would place stones inside the uterus of their female camels prior to long trips across the desert.

Through the centuries this idea persisted, and many kinds of objects have been placed inside the uterus to prevent pregnancy. Apparently, all of these objects were prone to cause infection, so in modern time, beginning about twenty years ago, new forms of IUDs, made in various shapes and from a variety of materials, were developed.

No one knows for sure how an IUD works to prevent pregnancy. It obviously is a foreign object in the cavity of the uterus and causes inflammation of the uterine lining. Some think that it hinders pregnancy by preventing a fertilized egg from implanting in the uterus, either because of that inflammation or by causing a mechanical "miniabortion." Some think that its presence causes the tube to increase its activity and propel a fertilized egg into the uterus too fast, making it arrive there before it is capable of implanting. Some think it interferes with the migration of sperm through the uterus into the tube.

No one knows, either, how the IUD causes infections in the uterus, tubes, or ovaries (or all of these), but one thing is indisputable and has been proven over and over again: Women who use IUDs develop pelvic infections significantly more often than those who don't.

When I was in my specialty training the IUD was relatively new and looked like a promising answer to the need for an effective alternative to the birth-control pill, which was then beginning to cause concern over its side effects. The IUD appeared to have a failure rate of less than 2 percent, and it needed essentially no attention after it had been inserted into the uterine cavity.

As the years went by, and the body of experience with the IUD grew, gynecologists were treated to many published studies about the effectiveness of the IUD and about the complications that it could cause. Most of these studies were funded and/or performed by the drug companies that made and sold the IUDs. After a while there were a number of types of IUDs in use, and physicians were told in the literature produced by the drug companies that the IUD could fail, could cause abnormal bleeding, could result in tubal pregnancy if pregnancy occurred, and could cause cramps. On rare occasions, they said, serious pelvic infection could occur while the IUD was in place, and it should be removed while this was treated and then be replaced. They also mentioned that if the physician should insert it inexpertly, it might perforate the uterus and have to be retrieved by an operation.

The above is intended not to be an exact description of the

literature but to give you an idea of the tone of the warnings and advice provided to physicians in the pamphlets, articles, and other sources upon which physicians are dependent for drug and device information.

As I gained practical experience with IUDs, I encountered everything that I had been told could go wrong with them, and much, much more. I saw more than one patient close to death from terrible pelvic infections, with ovarian abscesses, pelvic abscesses, blood clots in the pelvic veins. Some patients survived only after removal of the uterus, tubes, and ovaries and long hospitalizations with massive doses of intravenous antibiotics. I saw more than one patient with bowel obstruction caused by an IUD that had perforated the uterus long after it was inserted, and many times I removed from the abdominal cavity an IUD that had perforated the uterus, the removal being done either through a laparoscope or an incision.

During this time, I saw innumerable patients with abnormal bleeding, cramps, pelvic pain, and painful intercourse associated with the IUD. In fact, in my group practice we began to keep a log of all the IUDs we removed because of such symptoms, but we soon abandoned that effort because there were so many cases that it was not practical. In those days, infertility was not a large part of my practice, but even then I saw a significant number of patients with infertility due to scarred fallopian tubes who had no significant history other than the previous use of an IUD. There was nothing unusual about my practice or my group, so I have to assume that other physicians were seeing the same things. In 1977, I decided that I could never in good conscience insert another IUD.

It's now, finally, common and public knowledge that the Dalkon Shield IUD had become such an obvious cause of pelvic infections that it was removed from the market by A. H. Robins, the drug company that produced it and that had long protested its innocence. The company has since filed for bankruptcy and is in the process of settling out of court the hundreds of lawsuits filed against it by patients harmed by the device.

While the Dalkon Shield was being scrutinized by the public, the government, and the scientific community, more and more studies were being done, and published, about the complications of IUDs in general. Essentially all of them confirmed that women who used IUDs were at greater risk of developing pelvic infections. Though the greatest risk appeared to be associated with the Dalkon Shield, the risk clearly increased with all types of IUDs. In the majority of these studies, though, the conclusion stated that the actual cause was still not known, and that most probably the infections were related to sexually transmitted disease, and thus really the fault of the patients themselves.

My feeling at the time was that the risk was great enough to warrant the removal from the market of all IUDs. Many people nonetheless felt that it was such an effective contraceptive device that the complications were acceptable, given the need both in Third World countries and in ours for birth control that is not dependent for its effectiveness on the individual's reliable use of it day in and day out.

I've always disagreed with medical and ethical arguments that discount the individual because of the "greater good" for the population at large, and I didn't like this one either. If the IUD was to still be approved for use, I felt, every patient who had one inserted should at least be making an informed choice. She should know that she might die from the IUD or might never have an uncomfortable symptom until years after insertion, when she could find that she had been rendered incurably sterile by it. Indeed, she should be told about every possible side effect in such a way that she could understand and believe that it *could* happen to her.

* * *

In 1980 I was contacted by a local attorney and asked if I would come to a lunch meeting about IUDs with an attorney from another city. I respected the attorney's manner of handling medical malpractice litigation, and I agreed to come.

The attorney I met was involved with a large number of suits against the G. D. Searle Company and with the nationwide sharing of expert information concerning the Copper-7 IUD (a Searle product) and its damage to users. Although she actually had an engineer doing studies on the Copper-7 to try to determine the mechanism by which it caused pelvic infections, she and other attorneys had difficulty getting reputable physicians to testify on behalf of the patients. Since these cases were not malpractice cases against the physicians who had inserted the IUDs but suits against the company that manufactured the devices, I was reluctant to get involved. I felt that I was not an expert on their research procedures or their possible liability in marketing a birth-control device that might have possible dangerous side effects.

The attorney was understanding about this, but asked me not to make a decision until I'd had a chance to review various documents. These she provided; they included Searle internal company memos, research protocols, unpublished research data, instructions to the physicians who did the clinical studies on the Copper-7, and letters between some of these physicians and the Searle personnel. What I discovered was that there had been early evidence of problems with the Copper-7, and that the research protocols were constructed in such a way that physicians doing clinical trials of the IUD had no way to note certain side effects on the reporting forms. I learned that warnings from Searle researchers had been ignored by people in charge of the research project.

Over the course of the next two years I saw many women

referred to me by the attorney, some as patients, some only for me to examine them and to review their records. For most of them I became involved, as an expert witness, in their lawsuits against the Searle Company. None of these suits were against physicians, and the issues were clear and consistent in each case. Did the Copper-7 IUD cause pelvic infections in some of the women who used them and did the Searle Company have knowledge of this and deliberately prevent its disclosure? The answers were clear in my mind, but the legal tactics the defense attorneys used against these women had little to do with a search for truth.

My testimony was always the same: that I had seen many patients with pelvic infections that had no identifiable cause other than the Copper-7; that the patient in question had sustained tubal damage which, to a reasonable degree of medical probability, was caused by her use of a Copper-7; and that I did not believe that the information provided by Searle to doctors and to patients adequately informed patients of the risks involved with the use of the Copper-7.

I also testified that, in my expert opinion, the gynecological research literature documented the correlation between Copper-7 use and pelvic infection. I couldn't testify that I knew exactly how it occurred, because I didn't. The approach taken by the attorneys representing Searle was not usually focused upon proving that the Copper-7 did not cause pelvic infections, because they couldn't do that. Rather, they tried to suggest that something else was the cause, and they believed that sexually transmitted infections were the best bet. This led them to use questions that probed the plaintiff's sexual and marital history, searching for any possible source of infection. If they found none, their purpose was still served by this line of questioning. Basically, the effect was to intimidate and assault the character of the woman involved, much as is done in the defense of rapists.

If these attorneys could show the female plaintiff how awful her appearance in court might be, they could sometimes make her withdraw her suit. If this failed, the standard tactic was to suggest that the patient's pelvic infection had been caused by venereal disease. Since in none of these cases in which I was involved had a woman been previously shown to be a victim of venereal disease, the attorneys focused on questions of how many sex partners she had experienced in her life, at what ages, in what ways, and how frequently with each.

They loved to discuss it in court if the woman had previously had an abortion, and they even dwelled on such "shady" history as yeast infections, or the presence of the word "discharge" in a medical record. They hoped to suggest to an uninformed jury that these things might have something to do with subsequent tubal damage. The husband was subjected to the same line of questioning in an attempt to suggest that he had brought an infection to his wife from some other woman. In one case, the attorney tried to make a case for this based on one sexual experience the husband had had at age seventeen. If they could get the woman to admit to any marital troubles, arguments, or separations, they used this to suggest that it had probably reflected underlying infidelity and, thus, unknown venereal disease brought in from outside the marriage. The attorneys knew that the research literature documented a higher incidence of infection in IUD wearers. It was their view that these women, as a group, were somehow different, perhaps in their sexual habits, and that the difference explained the higher frequency of infection.

If all else failed, they tried to use this kind of testimony to suggest that perhaps the couple didn't have intercourse often enough to get pregnant, or that they really didn't want or deserve children, so, of course, the IUD hadn't really done much harm. In one case, where the woman was not only infertile but had required removal of her uterus, tubes, and ovaries, they tried to suggest that this had not really harmed her either, but had in fact improved her life.

After I had done a number of legal depositions of this kind, one of my partners received a phone call from a gynecologist of his acquaintance in Denver, sixty miles to the north. This doctor told my partner that he had heard there was a gynecologist in Colorado Springs who had become a "plaintiff's whore," and he wondered if my partner knew this guy, John Smith. My partner informed him that I was in fact one of his partners and that I was not the kind of person who would lie under oath for money. This gentleman suggested that I be told that the word was out about me in the gynecologic community and that I should be encouraged to lay off the drug company and to stay away from plaintiffs' lawyers.

I later had an opportunity to read this man's deposition from a case in which I was not involved and in which he testified as an expert for Searle. He stated that he had never seen a research article that, to his mind, indicated a correlation between IUDs and pelvic infections; that as far as he was concerned, the Copper-7 did not cause any serious side effects; and that he encouraged its use for anyone needing contraception. This statement was so ignorant of the facts that it could not have been made in good faith by a board-certified gynecologist, as this man was, and I had to believe that his motives included something other than a search for the truth or concern for the welfare of women.

I was a little surprised that physicians would see this kind of legal case as a threat to them and would try to obstruct it as they do medical malpractice cases. Many physicians feel that if a fellow physician, especially one in their own specialty, is threatened with a suit, it could just as well be them the next time, so they refuse to render an honest opinion. They also fear, more and more, that any judgment against a physician will ultimately increase malpractice-insurance premiums, so they feel justified in their lack of cooperation.

It has always seemed to me that honest and appropriate opinions about medical cases would help weed out bad physicians and protect good ones, and thus not only protect the public but eventually reduce malpractice premiums. I admit that I have had little support for this argument from other physicians, and both patients and attorneys must deal with a significant conspiracy of silence.

But the IUD questions were different than malpractice suits because physicians were not being threatened at all. The issue was one of safety for their patients and, in this case, there was also the question of whether physicians can rely on the information provided to them by a drug company about its products. I suppose for some of them it's just a matter of including all things medical within the Brotherhood, and acting in such a way as to protect each other at all costs, even when the cost is to their patients.

In the past, I have been vaguely threatened by physicians for rendering opinions in malpractice cases, even when the physicians involved didn't know what opinion I had rendered and when, indeed, I had actually supported the physician's treatment. In fact, in a majority of the cases I have reviewed for an attorney, I have prevented a suit from being filed by giving my honest opinion that no medical negligence or error was involved. I believe that if all physicians were willing to testify honestly about whether there was or was not negligence in a tentative suit, much of the malpractice nightmare would be over.

Nevertheless, I have reason to believe that now, more than ever, physicians in various states (perhaps all of them) are being pressured by malpractice-insurance carriers to refrain from giving expert opinion against another physician who uses the same insurance. This pressure is articulated plainly in "private" meetings of physicians with insurance representatives who are speaking on "risk management." The strong suggestion is passed from physician to physician, having originated, I have been told, with lawyers for the insurance companies. The threat to physicians is twofold: one, that their malpractice coverage could be canceled, and two, that premiums will go up for all doctors if everyone doesn't cooperate in this obstruction of the patient's rights. I will admit here that I cannot prove this, since part of "risk management" apparently involves not putting such things in writing.

Where is the patient in all this? Totally disregarded and kept largely in the dark because of the complete autonomy and authority that physicians in our country have managed to acquire. Virtually no other professionals can function with so little light shed on their activities. No other professionals have the opportunity to control the activities that are designed to ensure quality and protect the consumer. No other professionals can have such control over their charges and income, and no other professionals have been elevated to a position where their pronouncements are accepted as fact, whether they know what they're talking about or not.

Returning to Jan's story, I attempted a laser microsurgical repair on her tubes and managed to get them open. They remained open for several years. As is true with the majority of these IUD-damaged tubes, however, getting them open doesn't mean they will function, and Jan has been unable to become pregnant. Jan is one of the approximately seven hundred women with lawsuits filed against Searle, which has now removed the Copper-7 from the market. All of these suits will eventually be settled, Jan's along with the rest. In the meantime, the legal system will only add to the suffering of these women who have already been abused, and few doctors will be on their side.

Considering all the possible forms of contraception, my recommendation concerning the IUD is unequivocal: Don't use one! There are very few still on the market, but the old argument—that it is a good contraceptive for "the masses" and that its statistical safety justifies its use—has recently been resurrected. In fact, the old studies are being reexamined, and research articles are now being published which conclude that the problem with IUDs has always been that women who wear them *and contract a sexually transmitted disease* may get infection spread to the tubes and ovaries. These articles suggest that the IUD is safe for monogamous women with no infidelity in the relationship who have also been proven free from chlamydial and other infections. I am not even close to being convinced, though I will admit that appropriate, honest research may find the path to a safe form of IUD. My opinion, for now, remains that an individual virtually always has better choices.

In defense of doctors, most acted in good faith in the IUD controversy because they had faith in what they read in their medical journals and they had faith in the drug companies. On the other hand, they failed to put the patient first and to consider, on the patient's behalf, that their faith might be misplaced. This demonstrates the influence of the Brotherhood phenomenon and shows that male doctors have prejudices that often prevent them from giving women the benefit of the doubt, and from applying appropriate skepticism to things that originate within the male-oriented medical-scientific community.

Twelve

MY PATIENTS
NEVER ASK
ABOUT SEX

MOST PATIENTS ASSUME THAT IF A DOCTOR IS TALKING, HE MUST KNOW what he's talking about. In my experience, doctors are loath to admit to ignorance about any subject, but especially about anything that should be within their area of expertise. Here are two examples of doctors' attempts to deal with their ignorance in some way other than admitting to it.

Late one afternoon I went into the physicians' on-call room at the hospital. There I found a fellow gynecologist, whom I will call Fred, along with a uniformed police officer. Fred was terrified. It seems that one of his patients had called the hospital to say that her husband was on his way with a gun, and with plans to shoot him. As it turned out, this incident was caused not by Fred's inability to solve the patient's medical problems, but by his first professional attempt at sex counseling!

It was the 1970s, and even though Masters and Johnson had published their first research on human sexuality in 1966, none of us had been exposed to any education about sexuality or sex counseling in medical school or during internship.

Fred, however, had experienced some significant marital problems himself, centered around sex, and somehow had been motivated to begin attending X-rated movies with his wife. He felt this experience had freed them both from their inhibitions; that had led

97

to better sexual experiences together, and then to a happier marriage. Because of this, he began advising any patient who complained about sexual difficulties or who asked questions about sex to attend one of the local porno theaters. It wasn't long before he recommended this to a woman whose husband was somewhat volatile and who saw Fred's advice as an indecent suggestion—thus the gun and the threat.

The plainclothes police officers spread themselves around the hospital, easily spotted the agitated husband, and disarmed and arrested him. The whole incident would have been hilarious if we had not all been aware that during the previous week a physician in an emergency room in Canada had been shot and killed by an insanely jealous husband who couldn't tolerate his wife's having been examined by the gynecologist.

Years later, in my own office, a patient named Dorothy came to see me with what was a very common array of complaints regarding sex. She had little interest in sex, responded little or not at all during intercourse, had never experienced orgasm, and only engaged in sex to please her husband. She wanted to know if there was a medical reason for this, and if anything could be done to improve the situation. She had already been to see Dr. Ames, another gynecologist, and was still angry about that encounter.

A very prim and proper lady, Dorothy weighed something over two hundred pounds and was miserably uncomfortable even talking about her body, or about sex. Only pressure from her husband had taken her to a doctor to discuss it. She saw herself as failing at something that she believed other people found easy and natural, and she felt she was falling short in her responsibility to her husband, whom she loved very much.

Dr. Ames, like Fred, had experienced some marital problems that he felt were due to boredom with sex. Influences unknown to me had convinced him that the missing ingredient was oral sex, and he and his wife began an intense program of various forms of oral stimulation (I know about this because he spoke of it frequently in the surgeons' lounge). He experienced such a reawakening of sexual pleasure in his marriage that he felt it was the answer for everyone. He became a sort of champion of oral sex and, I was told, began to recommend it to colleagues and prescribe it for patients. When Dorothy appeared in his office, he gave her a long, detailed, and graphic description of the joys and techniques of oral sex. She had never heard of such things and was embarrassed, humiliated, and frightened; Dr. Ames told her she was a prude and just needed to loosen up. Needless to say, she didn't stay around long, and it surprises me that she ever motivated herself to see another gynecologist.

Two doctors, years apart in time, twenty years apart in age, and both had so little knowledge about basic human sexuality and sex counseling that they simply recommended what they thought had worked for them. I guess these doctors' patients were lucky that they hadn't personally obtained positive results from narcotics, or brain surgery.

Knowledge about human sexuality is now widely available, and today some medical schools even offer courses concerning these areas, but the majority of gynecologists continue to be totally unwilling, or unable, to competently meet the needs that their patients bring to them regarding their sexuality.

When I began my own practice, I soon realized that I was hopelessly inadequate to deal with the sexual questions and problems presented to me by my patients. I traveled to South Carolina for a postgraduate training program in sex therapy. It was a terrific experience and proved to be of more practical value than almost anything in my clinical training.

Back home, I offered to share what I had learned with my partners, and set up a series of sessions with them. They weren't wildly enthusiastic, but they went through with it politely. I never knew whether it resulted in changes in the way they responded to their patients, except for one of them, who made it quite clear that it wasn't going to change *him.*

One of the older partners, he became somewhat angry during the first session. Essentially, he told me that he thought the whole business about sex, and sex therapy, was ridiculous. His feeling was that this was just another new fad that had no lasting value for medical practice, and he wondered who had made up the notion that patients needed to talk about sex with their doctors. Maybe *my* practice was different, he said to me, but *his* patients *never* asked about sex!

To understand how his practice experience could be so different from that of other physicians, you have to understand how he and many others structure the doctor-patient interaction so as to limit the patient's opportunity, or desire, to discuss sensitive issues. Some physicians actually question their patients in a setting where only a curtain separates them from other patients. One physician of my acquaintance had a more appropriate physical setting than that, but he created his own emotional barriers.

When a patient came to his office she would be greeted by a nurse, who would question her as to the reason for the visit, then give her the typical skimpy office gown and leave her to undress. Since she was managing three exam rooms this way, the nurse made it clear by her manner and her questions that she had no time for lengthy discussion.

The patient would see the doctor after she had donned the gown and waited for some time. He would enter the room and greet her as he simultaneously laid her down and placed her feet in the stirrups. After completing the exam, he usually made some hasty remarks like "everything's fine, see you next year," then left the room. If he wanted to suggest surgery, he usually made his pitch after the patient had dressed, and if the patient agreed to have an operation scheduled, the nurse took over with scheduling and instructions while he moved on to another room.

Obviously, if you want someone to discuss sensitive, personal problems or worries, you create a setting and a mood in which this can comfortably occur. The reasons why this is so seldom done are many, and some have to do with the fact that gynecologists are just people, with the same array of attitudes about sex as the rest of the population, and with the same variance in level of comfort about discussing it. Other reasons have to do with the expense of adequate office design and staffing and with the lack of increased income produced by spending additional time with a patient.

In the 1960s, when Masters and Johnson first appeared on the program of the annual clinical meeting of the American College of Obstetrics and Gynecology to present their research on human sexual response, they were essentially ejected from the meeting by the gynecologists gathered there. Because Masters and Johnson were presenting film documentation of sexual physiologic response and had used prostitutes and volunteers to make the films, the gynecologists attending the meeting felt the researchers' work to be indecent and inappropriate for their consideration. Prior to Masters and Johnson's research, knowledge of human sexual response was essentially nonexistent. They pioneered basic research over two decades, studying the sexual behavior of men and women under scientific laboratory conditions. Their studies led to an understanding of the basic physiology of human sexual response, and they described it in detail in *Human Sexual Response,* published in 1966.

Today, most of our society accepts human sexuality as a normal part of human behavior, but I am still disappointed that gynecologists as a group did not lead the way to this reasonable and healthy attitude. What they had rejected at that initial, historic meeting was no less than the first accurate information about hu-

101

man sexual response, one of the last totally unknown areas of human physiology. If anyone should have understood its importance and its value, it was the group of gynecologists gathered there. Instead, they demonstrated, not for the last time, that they were no more special, sensitive, or wise than the rest of the male population. In a book titled *Obstetrics and Gynecology in America: A History,* published by the American College of Obstetrics and Gynecology and written by Harold Speert, the names of Masters and Johnson do not even appear in the index! Neither do the words *sexuality* or *orgasm,* and in a chapter titled "Some Physiologic Trailblazers," Masters and Johnson are not mentioned. This book was written in 1980.

Besides the fact that many male gynecologists simply are not comfortable with their own sexuality, much less that of their patients, there are many who remain quite ignorant about sex and couldn't answer their patients' questions if their own lives depended on it. Those men are not going to try to provide opportunities for their patients to discuss sex. Those who had no formal education about human sexuality during their medical school and specialty training must travel, at significant expense of time and money, to attend a postgraduate training program if they are to become even minimally knowledgeable about the subject. Many are not willing to admit that they need further education in something that should already be a part of their repertoire, and many are too uncomfortable about sex to tolerate the experience of the course.

Like almost everything that involves physicians, there is also an economic explanation. For a surgical specialist like a gynecologist, the less time spent in the office, listening and communicating, and the more time in the operating room, the greater will be the yearly income. This fact is responsible for the increasing use of videotape machines, pamphlets, and other office-management techniques designed to move patients in and out as quickly as possible and to lessen the time that the patients have access to the doctor.

There is no justification for any of this. When a patient comes to see a primary-care physician, she brings with her all kinds of needs. Not just the need to have medical illness diagnosed and treated, but also the need for information, for reassurance, for advice about a healthy life-style and about marital problems, and for education about her body and her sexuality. Physicians who want to be primary-care resources for women have to be able to meet all these needs. They do not have the right to pretend to be there for that purpose but actually to be filtering through a lot of patients, culling out those that provide large chunks of income by having surgery and shortchanging the rest.

Many, many women live with self-doubt, guilt, depression, and marital difficulties or miss the experience of giving and receiving sexual pleasure simply because they have not been fortunate enough to encounter a primary-care physician caring and capable enough to address their sexual problems.

While some physicians will claim that they simply don't have the office time to take on sex-therapy patients or say that sex therapy is the proper role of psychiatrists, the truth is that almost all patients can have their sexual problems successfully addressed in a short time, and with little skill involved. As with obstetrical care, gynecologists are unwilling to give up control by allowing non-M.D.s to assume more responsibility, even though it would both solve their time problems and improve patient care. They retain the role of primary-care provider, but they neither become competent in sexual counseling nor refer patients to those who are. They define the concerns that are appropriate for their attention by their needs rather than yours.

The fact is, most sexual problems presented to a physician can be resolved with one of two things: *information* or *permission giv-*

ing. Many women need only to know how their body, or that of their sex partner, works; if their sexual functioning is normal; or if their anatomy is normal. Many others simply need to be told that it's O.K. for them to desire, or to think about, or to do the things that they already desire, think about, or do. They just need to be given permission, by someone seen as an authority, to experience and to enjoy normal sexual activities. It is a rare patient whose difficulties require psychotherapy or an organized, lengthy sex-therapy program, and those patients can easily be identified by physicians with a minimum of training, if they are willing to listen, and be referred to appropriate specialists.

The setting in which a woman should see a doctor is one in which there is complete privacy, so that she can feel comfortable while undressing and when the door is opened for a doctor or nurse to enter. It should provide a comfortable sense that no one outside can hear any conversation. If the doctor wants to be the person with whom a patient is to discuss her problems or questions, then it should be the doctor who asks, not the nurse or the medical assistant or a computer. The doctor should also create an atmosphere of openness, a sense of available time, and a feeling of interest and caring. Obviously, the time a patient must be undressed should be minimized, and she should be greeted while dressed and given the chance to talk while dressed, as well.

It takes so little to create the proper setting that any physicians who do not take the trouble should be suspected of a degree of insensitivity that probably reaches into all other areas of their practice.

The word *doctor* comes from the Latin word *doctor,* the original meaning of which was "teacher." In the area of sexuality, as in others, the teachers have not only failed to teach, they have failed to learn.

The best way to approach your doctor about sexual matters is simply to ask, "Now that we have covered everything else, may I ask you some questions about sex?" If your physician genuinely does not have the time, ask if you can set up an appointment specifically for that purpose. Most of the time, you will only need some factual information about your sexual response or your partner's, your anatomy or his, the appropriateness of your expectations about orgasm, the safety of some sexual practice, the degree to which you engage in a particular sexual activity, or whether you experience or don't experience something. If your doctor doesn't seem willing or able to talk about these things, or genuinely feels you need an experienced sex counselor, by all means find one.

Most of the time sexual concerns, or perceived sexual problems in a relationship, are reflections of problems with the relationship itself. Most often, once you have learned that you have no physical barrier to the enjoyment of sex, the appropriate help to be sought will be from a psychotherapist or marriage counselor. In cases of problems that are clearly sexual only, existing within a good relationship, a sex-therapy clinic or a sex therapist certified by the American Association of Sex Educators, Counselors and Therapists is the place to turn.

Within the category of sexual problems I would include such things as male psychological impotence, the physical inability of a woman to allow vaginal penetration (vaginismus), inability to experience orgasm from any type of stimulation, or total sexual unresponsiveness in someone who would like to respond.

A last bit of advice: Do not ever let a physician convince you that surgery of any kind can improve your sexual pleasure. Such things as clitoral circumcision or "tightening" of the vagina will not bring about the kind of results that some gynecologists will claim. In fact, many operations on the vagina can have the unfortunate side effect of lessening vaginal sensation, and hysterectomy or vaginal repair can result in such a shortened vagina that intercourse may be uncomfortable forever.

The only time that surgery can have a positive effect on female sexual response is when it eliminates a disease process that has caused so much pain with intercourse that pleasure has been short-circuited and orgasm prevented. This happens more often with endometriosis than with any other disorder, though complete prolapse of the uterus, in which the uterus has totally lost its tissue support and protrudes through the vaginal opening, may make satisfactory intercourse virtually impossible.

Sexuality is just as normal, and just as female, as menstruation and should be addressed as such by any physician who is likely to meet your needs in other areas.

Thirteen

A HARSH JUDGMENT

A JUDGMENTAL ATTITUDE ABOUT ANY ASPECT OF WOMEN AND THEIR sexuality exists in some male gynecologists as well as in other men. When that attitude is brought to the office, the result can be seen both in bad diagnoses and treatment and in humiliating and demeaning behavior toward a patient.

Evelyn had just moved to town and was in the midst of all the stressful things that accompany a move. She not only had to get settled into a new house and get her children started in a new school, she had to set up a new professional office. She was never daunted by a challenge, though, and was more than capable of taking care of herself and her children, as she had done since her divorce, but her life was about to change permanently, altered by something new and totally unexpected.

When she first noticed the tingling and burning near the opening of her vagina, she wondered if she had pinched herself somehow. Within a couple of days, though, the burning became very intense, and she couldn't sit comfortably or wear jeans. She also felt feverish, tired, and weak.

Using a mirror, she managed to get a good look at the area of her labia that hurt. The area was swollen and red, and in the middle of it was a place that looked like a small crater. Evelyn had absolutely no idea what she was seeing and was justifiably worried. She had gone through her two pregnancies with no problems, and she had never experienced any kind of gynecologic problems. Being new to town she also had no physician, and not a clue how to choose the best gynecologist.

The phone book seemed her best source of information, so she looked in the Yellow Pages and chose Dr. Altman. Having no other basis on which to make a choice, she picked a gynecologist whose office was conveniently located.

After a ninety-minute wait, the nurse took her into an examination room and left her there to fill out a medical-history questionnaire. Twenty minutes later she came back and told Evelyn to undress completely, put on a paper gown, and wait. As time went by, Evelyn tried to suppress the anger she was feeling, as well as the thought that an affluent and well-educated woman should get better treatment than she was getting. She knew that her credentials really had nothing to do with it, that no one should be treated that way. She told herself that the doctor was surely busy and, after all, had worked her in for an appointment right away.

When he finally arrived, Dr. Altman spent little time getting to know his new patient. After determining that she had one problem, the painful, swollen area on her vaginal opening, he proceeded to do a breast exam, a pelvic exam, and a Pap smear, then told her to get dressed and left the room.

While she waited, Evelyn tried to imagine what she was going to be told. Altman had seemed calm enough, so surely there was nothing serious going on. She just wanted a diagnosis, a prescription, and to get out of there.

When he came back, Dr. Altman sat down and said, "Well, you've got a herpes infection, but it's surely not the worst one I've seen, and after the first one, it usually isn't as bad in the future." Evelyn had no idea what he was talking about.

"What is it?" she asked.

"Well, it's a viral infection. You get it by having sex with someone who has it."

"How do you treat it?"

"There isn't any treatment: once you've got it, you'll keep it for life. It'll come and go, and if you have sex with someone else they'll get it from you; there's no cure. Why don't you try some warm sitz baths. It'll probably get better, this time, in about two weeks."

Evelyn couldn't believe he was getting up to leave. "Wait a minute, I don't understand any of this, I need to know a lot more than you've told me."

Dr. Altman became irritated. "Look honey," he said. "This is the price you pay for sleeping around. Get a pamphlet from the nurse on your way out. You have plenty of time to learn about herpes, a lot longer than it took you to get it." With that, he left, and Evelyn sat there with her emotions boiling over. Anger, fear, confusion overwhelmed her. She almost ran from the office.

It took her three days to find another doctor who would see her right away just to talk. During that time, she was almost immobilized by her feelings. All she understood from what Dr. Altman had told her was that she had some kind of incurable disease and that she could never have sex again. The pamphlet gave her the basic facts: herpes simplex was a sexually transmitted virus that lived in people's tissues and periodically erupted as a painful sore. While the sore was there, the pamphlet said, the virus could easily be given to a sex partner. There was no cure. The brochure didn't begin to answer all her questions, much less give her any reassurance.

Evelyn told me much later that during this time she felt so bad about herself, so hopeless about her life, that she seriously contemplated suicide. It took a lot of time, a lot of information, a lot of accepting interaction to help her get to where she is today. She still has herpes, but she accepts it as an unfortunate consequence of normal, acceptable, responsible, and meaningful sexual relations with a man who unknowingly carried what was then a little-known infection. Had she first seen a competent, caring, sensitive, empathetic physician, she could have been spared a great deal of pain.

Sexually transmitted disease is a fact of life. The term once meant syphilis or gonorrhea; today it also means herpes, chlamydia, hemophilus, condylomata acuminata, AIDS, and others. The diagnosis and treatment of these infections are an everyday experience for a gynecologist. *How* a woman is told about any of these is at least as important as *what* she is told. But, as in the case of Evelyn and Dr. Altman, the patient is often subjected to the doctor's prejudices, moral judgments, sexual hang-ups, or personal inadequacy. This is clearly unacceptable, but this kind of behavior occurs frequently in a more subtle manner. When a doctor's prejudicial attitudes or sexist behavior is not dramatically displayed, the patient may often question the accuracy of her perception of the event, giving the doctor the benefit of any doubt. Just as with inappropriate sexual remarks or physical action by a gynecologist, trust your instincts and your judgment. These kinds of behaviors *do* occur in the sanctity of gynecologists' offices. If you think it happened, it almost certainly did.

Fourteen

ONE OF THE BEST

THE RISE OF THE MEDICAL PROFESSION TO ITS CURRENT POSITION OF respect, authority, and autonomy developed at a time and in an environment where society was ridding itself of quackery and fraud. By making physicians unquestionable, almost godlike, we have provided an opportunity for fraud and deceit to again go unchecked. Some of the worst doctors I know have the reputation of being the best around, for a variety of reasons, none of which has anything to do with competence, honesty, or sensitivity.

A perfect example was Dr. Fairley. One afternoon a number of years ago I saw a very unhappy patient named Brenda who had already been evaluated and advised by him. Dr. Fairley had seen Brenda for irregular menstrual periods and pain and had performed a laparoscopy. After this operation Dr. Fairley had told Brenda that she had, at some time in her past, had a severe infection involving her reproductive organs, and that it had essentially destroyed them. He recommended that she let him remove her uterus, tubes, and ovaries, and told her that there was no other way to relieve her pain and irregular periods.

Brenda was willing to go along with the operation because Dr. Fairley had also told her that it was impossible for her to ever become pregnant. However, she was a little distressed at the prospect of having her ovaries removed and asked him if he could just take out her uterus and try to save her ovaries. His response was quite firm. There was no way, he told her, to salvage her ovaries, or to treat her situation in any other way at all. For this reason she came to me, asking that I do her surgery and try to salvage all that I could.

Even though I would have preferred to try to repair her tubes and ovaries, Brenda was quite adamant that she did not want to ever get pregnant again; besides, Dr. Fairley had convinced her that without surgery she would have pain and abnormal periods for the rest of her life.

I agreed to obtain Dr. Fairley's dictated operative summary before making a decision. When I did, the findings could not have been described more clearly. He described both fallopian tubes as being completely blocked, filled with fluid, and distended like small balloons; he said the ovaries, uterus, tubes, and intestines were adhered together. It was such a hopeless picture that anyone would have given Brenda essentially no hope of future pregnancy, even with a skillful attempt at microsurgical repair of the damage.

Planning to conserve some or all of at least one ovary, I proceeded with surgery on Brenda, prepared for hours of attempting to deal with the massive adhesions and the rest of the terribly distorted anatomy that Dr. Fairley had described. But at the operating table I found a perfectly normal set of reproductive organs. The tubes and ovaries were free of adhesions or abnormality, and the rest of the structures in the pelvis were normal and certainly had never been involved in an infection or any other disease.

I had never been angrier. Brenda recovered from the relatively small incision normally, but I had done a totally useless operation!

Over the years I saved records of cases in which Dr. Fairley's findings at laparoscopy were subsequently discovered to be completely inconsistent with reality. You can be sure that I never operated on anyone again on the strength of someone else's laparoscopy, especially his, because I wound up with a drawerful of these cases. I never knew whether he was totally incompetent to do a laparoscopy, simply made up findings, or was so dishonest that he falsified findings to support the recommendation of a subsequent hysterectomy. I'm still unable to think of any other possible explanations.

Over the years I have heard, through the medical and legal grapevines, about an extraordinary number of serious surgical complications caused by Dr. Fairley, as well as a number of out-of-court settlements of malpractice suits based on substandard care.

Several years ago I got a call from the head of the ob-gyn department of a major medical center about a patient whom he wanted to refer to me for surgery. She had a large tumor of the ovary, and this physician expressed dismay that Dr. Fairley had not found it when he performed a laparoscopy on her one month earlier. "John," he said, "this tumor is *huge*. How could Dr. Fairley have missed it, when I understand he's one of the best!"

In fact, he's one of the worst. I could have filled this section on case histories with stories from his practice alone. But nothing has happened to change his good reputation, because nothing that he has done has been made public in any way. His malpractice suits have been quietly settled out of court. If there is a file on him with the State Board of Medical Examiners, it is not open to patients, and if his record of unnecessary surgery and surgical complications is unparalleled, as I suspect it is, the facts and figures have never been compiled and made available to patients who deserve to know more about this man than that he has a "good reputation."

In order to understand who gynecologists are and how they function, and thus how to appropriately interact with them to your best advantage, it is necessary to know how they are trained, how they obtain and retain their credentials, and how they interact with hospitals, clinics, one another, and the entities that pay their bills. So in the beginning of the next section I'll dedicate a chapter to describing these things.

SECTION THREE

Empowering Women

Fifteen

THE TRAINING OF A GYNECOLOGIST

WOMEN SELDOM CONCERN THEMSELVES WITH HOW OR WHY A PARTICULAR doctor became a gynecologist, but they are vitally concerned about whether he or she became a quality gynecologist. Too often, women rely on the gynecologist's "reputation," and if it appears to be good they assume that the gynecologist, too, is good.

How does someone get the reputation of being one of the "best" doctors of a particular kind, or in a particular locale? Most often doctors come by their reputations by telling people that they are good, or by having themselves represented as such by an interested party such as a hospital, their partner, their spouse, their office manager, their car dealer, anyone who benefits from that doctor doing a big business.

It's rare to hear information about how bad a doctor is, except from former patients, and they don't often have a large audience. It's much more common today to hear, in a hospital's advertisements for instance, that their staff physicians are all terrific, well-trained, caring, and attentive. I've listened to more than one hospital administrator, in private, tell me about the bad doctors on his staff, frauds, incompetents, obnoxious people, only to hear his radio ad the same week imploring the public to "Call our hot line, and let us help you find a quality physician." The list from which they choose, of course, includes every doctor who admits patients to that hospital. That's the source of their revenue, the only source, because patients cannot be admitted to a hospital without there being an admitting physician.

We seem to be inundated with helpful advice on how to find good medical care. On closer scrutiny you will find that it's not helpful at all. Every radio, T.V., and newspaper ad for hospitals, clinics, and insurance companies seems to have come from the same ad agency, the one that decided that they could sell anything in the world of medicine if they attached the word "caring" to it. It's as though by saying "we care," or that our doctors, nurses, lab techs, orderlies are all "caring people," hospitals can avoid having to explain their fees, their procedures for admitting physicians to their staffs, their infection rates, the frequency of unindicated surgery in their operating rooms, or the level of patient satisfaction with the food, the staff, the facilities, or the business office. There is a real product behind all this "caring" baloney. But when advertisers stop talking about the actual merits of a product and begin to talk in vague positive catchwords, you know there must be little of merit beneath those words. How long would we listen to, say, IBM telling us only that they're "nice" before we asked for some cost, quality, and service data?

Keeping in mind that they are not guarantees, there are a few significant labels and credentials that are helpful in the *initial* evaluation of a physician or hospital. The credentials can be thought of as landmarks along the path toward becoming a gynecologist, starting a practice, affiliating with hospitals, and establishing referral relationships with other physicians.

This chapter is a review of the education of a gynecologist. While it is true that some universities, medical schools, internship programs, and residency-training programs are better than others, it is also true that the basic educational experience of all gynecologists is essentially the same. It is also true that there are shortcomings common to most, if not all, gynecologists' education. I would like you to understand fully what your doctor's training may, and may not, have included, and what his or her credentials really tell you about him or her.

What I am about to describe will seem to most people like a great deal of education, training, and experience. Unfortunately, much of it is not what it seems. The process of educating physicians in America has gradually evolved to its current form, without a coherent "master plan" to guide it. If we could start from scratch and design the ideal educational process for the training of a gynecologist, the result would be significantly different from what exists today. It would be different because much of what we now have contributes little to the preparation of a college student for medical school, a medical student for specialty training, or a gynecology resident for being a woman's doctor. It would also be different because so much that would be appropriate preparation is not part of the existing process. As I describe the various stages, I'll point out some of the problems.

College

To enter an accredited medical school, a person has to complete a college curriculum that satisfies the requirements of the school. This curriculum has historically consisted of an undergraduate experience rich in science and poor in the arts, humanities, and business. The aspiring medical student obtains a Bachelor of Science degree, usually with a major in chemistry or biology, then applies to medical school.

Because it is not easy to get into medical school, most premedical college students concentrate on doing the minimum that is required as an undergraduate, so that their grades are as high as possible. This means that they usually avoid the "extra" courses that might make them genuinely educated people, and thus usually leave college without a broad-based education, often semiliterate (just read their office notes or hospital dictations), and usually with very narrow intellectual experience. Nothing in the later education of a physician significantly changes the basic intellectual makeup of the person he or she was at college graduation, and it is a rare physician who takes the time and trouble to broaden his or her horizons. Thus physicians tend to be people with brains capable of impressive memory feats, but are rarely skillful at functioning in the world outside medical practice.

Things have begun to change somewhat. Critics of the narrowness of physicians' perspectives of their patients and their patients' lives have questioned the adequacy of the education of a physician today. Medical schools have criticized the premedical education curriculum as providing them with something less than well-rounded human beings. As a result, admission standards are beginning to change, and many medical schools are admitting college graduates with degrees in nonscientific areas, such as the arts and humanities. The argument for this, of course, is that these people are bright enough to make up for whatever deficiencies they might have in areas such as chemistry and will be better raw material for the development of doctors who are capable of seeing their patients as something more than an array of scientific processes.

Paul Starr, in *The Social Transformation of American Medicine,* described the difficulties that American medical professionals faced as they tried to become credible. In large part, they achieved their goal by convincing society that medicine was rooted in complex and arcane science, and that physicians, through their education, had a grasp of that science which was unique to them as a group. It's ironic that we are beginning to see physicians as being less than they could be *because* they are too deeply rooted in science.

Medical School

Medical school is usually a four-year program, the first year being dedicated to the basic sciences, including anatomy, physiology, and biochemistry, and the second to more focused scientific areas, such as pathology, physical diagnosis, microbiology, and public health.

The second two years are the so-called clinical years, when students rotate among the various basic specialties of medical practice, internal medicine, surgery, orthopedics, ob-gyn, and pediatrics, as well as choosing elective time on subspecialty areas.

The basic science years are grueling, with enormous requirements for the memorization of a huge body of fundamental information. During this period a student scarcely has time to eat, sleep, and do laundry, let alone pursue intellectual diversion into unrelated areas. Medical students complain that what they are forced to learn is not germane to being a doctor, and the complaint has some merit. I remember well the trauma of taking the three-day basic-science portion of the National Board Examinations, which is the first half of a national test that can lead to licensure in most states. Fortunately, the test was administered at the end of my second year of medical school, when the incredible mass of basic science that I had crammed into my brain for the previous two years was still precariously balanced there. As it is with all physicians, I was never again asked to demonstrate my knowledge in those areas and, for the most part, used only a tiny fragment of it in subsequent medical practice.

When a medical student enters the last two years of medical school circumstances change dramatically, but there are still things to complain about. As they move through the various areas of clinical medicine, students must continue to study while being subjected to a work load that would make a galley slave tremble. The milieu in which a medical student labors encompasses a complete hierarchy of medicine: interns, first- through fourth-year residents, research fellows, and professors. Medical students are given a lot of work but little real responsibility, and they get no respect at all. Little wonder that they begin to develop the attitude that someday they will be at the top of the totem pole, will have paid their dues, and will deserve all that will justly come to them.

During this time, the medical student's world is the hospital, and there is little opportunity for experiencing life outside. That will not change in the internship and residency years to come. If elsewhere in this book I sound too critical of physicians for their lack of sensitivity, diversity, and personal depth, I should say that I am well aware that much of this is imposed on these basically bright people by the system of education and training that was not of their creation.

In the medical-education system there is virtually no attempt to teach the things that you wish your doctor had been taught: what it's like to be a patient, how to listen well, and how to approach the patient as a whole human being rather than a physiology lab or a disease that happens to occupy a person. There are efforts being made to introduce such things, as well as to teach would-be doctors the business aspects of medicine. These attempts are part of a wider discussion of curriculum reform in medical school and it is not yet clear how things will evolve.

Internship

At the end of medical school, the student graduates with an M.D. degree but cannot yet practice medicine. Before entering practice in any state, an M.D. must serve a year in an approved internship. This is done in a hospital or health-sciences center and basically consists of taking care of hospitalized patients while being supervised, further educated, and required to carry a major portion of the awesome work load that is the inevitable burden of teaching hospitals.

Long ago, everyone had essentially the same experience as an intern, but the age of specialization has changed that. Now a new M.D. must choose the type of internship he or she wants. It may be a general one, called a rotating internship, or a specialized one in a particular area of medical practice. These latter types are called straight internships, and they may be done in internal medicine, pediatrics, surgery, ob-gyn, or other specialties.

There is also an intermediate type of internship that focuses on a particular specialty, but with more general experience included. I, for instance, did a "rotating ob-gyn" internship, and six months of my year was spent in ob-gyn, the rest in surgery, internal medicine, anesthesiology, endocrinology, and gynecologic pathology, with a month in the emergency room.

As in medical school, there is no effort to teach an intern, who is seeing patients as a physician for the first time, how to see patients with a caring, sensitive, and empathetic manner. Worse, the lack of sleep and the huge volume of work combine to begin a process of depersonalization of the patient and dehumanization of the doctor that is continued in residency.

Residency

At the end of the internship a young doctor, at this point usually age twenty-seven or so, must choose whether to become a specialist or what used to be called a general practitioner. Those who choose the latter, to be G.P.s, must pass either a state licensing exam or the second (clinical) portion of the National Board Examination before beginning medical practice. Licensure to practice medicine is granted only for a specific state, though some states will accept the test results from certain other states and grant a license without further testing, and most states accept the National Board Exam. In 1992, the National Board Examination will be replaced by the United States Medical Licensing Exam (USMLE), and it will become the only examination pathway to medical licensure in the

United States. Thus, every new physician will take the same examination, but licensure will still be granted and renewed at the state level.

The same young physician may choose to become a general practitioner but go on to spend two years in a residency program for the *specialty* of general practice, which is now called family medicine. Once finished with the extra two years' training, the physician still will practice in a general way, caring for children, adult males, adult females, and the elderly but must obtain credentials in the specialty of family medicine in the same way as I will describe for the other specialties of medical practice.

An M.D. who wishes to be a specialist and restrict him- or herself to a particular area of medicine could theoretically simply obtain a medical license, hang out a shingle, and say that his or her practice will be limited to, say, ob-gyn. Very few people do that anymore because the risk of being successfully sued for malpractice is much greater if you haven't actually had the extra training required to specialize.

Prior to the 1930s, physicians who wished to become specialists could follow one of many routes, each of which involved additional training of some kind. There was not, however, any single path to specialization that was monitored or certified. A dual battle was going on at that time. Physicians were struggling to prevent people in other health-care occupations from being able to compete with them in the same marketplace. Thus, physicians were assailing lab and X-ray technicians, midwives, and others as being less worthy than themselves to function in an autonomous and entrepreneurial way. Simultaneously, within the field of medicine itself, doctors who considered themselves specialists were trying to characterize general practitioners as being in the same general category as some of their other opponents. Thus, for instance, the obstetrician alleged that the G.P. was no better qualified than a mid-wife to deliver babies.

In 1913, the AMA's Council on Medical Education recognized that there was a problem and recommended that the AMA regulate postgraduate schools. This was the beginning of a process that ultimately defined specialty training. But there was a majority of general practitioners in the AMA, and they resisted any action that would impair their ability to obtain hospital privileges to do any type of practice they wished in competition with specialists. The present system of certification by specialty boards (which I will describe later) developed outside the AMA in the 1930s. Even though it now clearly defines the specialties, there is no absolute power that resides in the boards that can prevent a general practitioner from practicing as a specialist. That, as I will describe, is regulated through systems that are more social than legal.

Today, the route to becoming a specialist in any area of medical practice is to go beyond internship into an approved residency program in your chosen field. The term "residency" was introduced in the early 1900s, when Johns Hopkins University used it to describe advanced specialty training following internship. The term now applies to a program that involves additional education and practical experience under supervision. Unlike internship, residency training is devoted entirely to the chosen specialty. There are many specialty areas, and most of them have subspecialty areas as well, but it will be easiest for me to focus on the specialty of gynecology.

Gynecology as a Specialty

Let's follow a young man who has finished an internship and decided that he wants to be a gynecologist. There are many theories, and many more bad jokes, about why a person chooses gynecology, but the factors underlying the decision are probably quite varied.

Gynecologists represent a wide spectrum of people, and their original primary motivations range widely as well.

In terms of conscious motivation, gynecologists might mention the attractiveness of a specialty that combines both surgical and nonsurgical activities. They might cite as positive the variation in type of activity that occurs within a workday, changing, as it does, from obstetrics to gynecology and from office to hospital.

There are also many negatives to the specialty, including the lack of control over when you work, where and how much you sleep, and whether you can schedule a workday uninterrupted by emergencies. The negatives are so oppressive that it is hard to believe that there are not some powerful subconscious motives that propel medical students toward choosing ob-gyn. After years of closely observing the personalities and behavior of gynecologists, I have to conclude that for many the subconscious motivation may involve the need to be in a powerful and controlling relationship with women. For the vast majority of gynecologists, though, I believe the decision to commit their lives to this specialty was made with conscious good intent and the belief that they were choosing to devote themselves to caring for women.

Whatever the reasons, the next step after internship is to enter into an ob-gyn residency program. The quality of residency programs in ob-gyn varies from academically excellent to mediocre. Guidelines for adequacy are set and monitored by the Council on Resident Education in Obstetrics and Gynecology, a body that represents the American Board of Obstetrics and Gynecology, the American College of Obstetrics and Gynecology, and four other organizations. It is this council that gives the stamp of approval to residency programs, and if a doctor wants to be recognized as a specialist and given the opportunity to be certified by the American Board of Obstetrics and Gynecology, he or she must complete one of the approved programs. Under the scrutiny of the Council, the number of approved programs had decreased from 495 in 1960 to 325 in 1975. At the same time, however, the number of physicians in such programs rose from 2,650 in 1960 to 3,652 in 1975.

In spite of the implication of the "approved" status, some residency programs regularly turn out a higher percentage of doctors who pass their board exams than do others, and interns know where in the hierarchy the various programs fall. Generally, the people who have been the best medical students and interns can get into the best residency programs.

Ob-gyn residencies are either three or four years in length and are roughly divided into equal parts of obstetrics and gynecology experience. Each year the level of responsibility and supervision changes, so we'll look at a typical progression of experience, but first let me delineate what is included in the medical specialty of ob-gyn.

Obstetrics is the specialty that deals with everything having to do with pregnancy, labor, and childbirth. It does not include care of infants once they have been born and turned over to the nursery or the pediatrician.

Gynecology is the specialty concerned with anything related to the reproductive system of women. It includes the diagnosis of all diseases of the reproductive organs and the treatment of those diseases, whether the treatment involves surgery or medication.

Ob-gyn is considered one specialty, and it is not possible to do a residency program in one or the other separately. Thus, anyone who has credentials in ob-gyn but practices only as an obstetrician or only as a gynecologist has chosen to abandon the practice of one or the other, after being trained in both. Those who bill themselves as being ob-gyn specialists more or less have to accept the role of being a primary-care physician to their patients. The American College of Obstetrics and Gynecology widely urged their constituents to accept that role when HMOs began seeking to define which physicians would be defined as primary care and which would be defined as specialists. In an HMO system a specialist can be paid for seeing a patient only when that patient is referred by a primary-care physician.

Within ob-gyn there are areas of subspecialty, for which there can be formalized training and credentialing after residency training. These include such things as gynecologic oncology (cancer treatment), infertility, endocrinology (treatment of hormonal disorders), and others. Generally, doctors who do fellowships in these subspecialty areas wind up as professors in teaching hospitals.

The first year of residency is much like an internship, though the first-year resident is slightly higher on the ladder of authority. He usually spends his obstetrical time in charge of a labor-and-delivery unit in a teaching hospital, standing twenty-four-hour shifts doing every delivery that occurs, or supervising interns and medical students learning how to do routine deliveries. In spite of the fact that he often will not sleep for the entire twenty-four hours, he usually has to stay at the hospital for the rest of the day, attending to the patients on the postpartum ward and seeing prenatal patients in the clinic. He then will go home for a night's sleep before coming back to do it again.

Most teaching hospitals are centers for indigent patients, so most training of interns and residents is done on women who cannot afford a private physician. Needless to say, the frequency of errors by these specialists-in-training is significantly higher the earlier in the training process the patient happens to encounter them.

The gynecologic portion of the first year consists of seeing patients in the clinic under supervision and assisting in surgery. Though the first-year residents usually get to do the simpler operations (D and C's, abortions, tubal ligations), they seldom get to do much else in the way of surgery, and most of them begin to count time and progress in terms of whether they have yet performed particular procedures.

Most of the resident's experience in doing common operations and complicated deliveries occurs during the second year. These procedures are done under the supervision of a senior resident or staff physician. The staff tends to be available for daytime, scheduled procedures, while the senior resident is in charge at night.

The last, or senior, year is mostly composed of teaching those lower in the hierarchy and having the chance to learn to perform unusual or especially difficult operations. The amount of opportunity available for this invaluable experience, and the exposure to really good surgical teachers, varies so greatly that some physicians come out of residency as accomplished, versatile surgeons, and others have barely seen most of the really challenging surgical situations. For instance, the experience of a resident in a hospital that treats mostly indigent patients will be quite different from that of his counterpart in a large academic referral center. These academic centers get fewer patients with common problems but are sent the rare, strange, and difficult cases that private physicians would rather not handle. This is but one of the ways that the character of a residency can vary.

The residents vary as well. Some residents, in fact, have so little natural ability to perform surgery (or any other skill requiring a modicum of manual dexterity) that they would not be capable surgeons regardless of the level of teaching they experienced. Others are such naturals that they can apply more limited experience to good effect and develop into accomplished surgeons with less repetition.

Notice that I've not described any education specifically about women, as opposed to education about women's anatomy and diseases. To my knowledge, there is still no attempt to teach gynecology residents about the unique needs of women, their perspective, their experience as patients, or (silly though it sounds) how they are different from men. Furthermore, you would think that within an institution that is devoted solely to the care of women, one that is teaching doctors to be exclusively doctors for women, there would be an aura of reverence and respect for women that would be almost palpable. In fact, sexism is no less prevalent in gynecologic residency programs than in any other male dominion, and in some ways it is more entrenched.

In the process of examining myself as a male and a gynecologist I have revisited, in my mind, my own internship and residency. What I recall is a barrage of sexist talk and behavior that has been unmatched by any definable experience since that time. If there is to be a major change in the attitudes of women's doctors, this is one of the places that it has to start!

Ob-Gyn Board Certification

Quality of attitude notwithstanding, if an entire residency has been completed, and that residency is one approved by the American Board of Obstetrics and Gynecology, the physician is now said to be "board-eligible." That means that he is eligible to become certified by the board, once certain prerequisites have been achieved.

First, the board-eligible physician must pass a written exam. Then he must collect information on all the surgery and deliveries he performs in private practice for two years. After that he travels to some large city for a lengthy oral examination administered by four ob-gyn specialists, usually full-time academic physicians (they teach and do research primarily, though many also do some private practice). If he passes this exam he is then (and forevermore) "board-certified," and thus an expert in the care of women.

Following the examination, the board-certified physician can apply to become a Fellow of the American College of Obstetrics and Gynecology. This involves paying significant fees, having two current fellows sign the application, and providing a copy of the board certification. As long as he keeps paying his dues, he will remain a fellow and be able to list himself as so-and-so, M.D., FACOG.

All of these steps having been successfully negotiated is good evidence of adequate training in the basics of the specialty, and the procedures are the same for all specialties, from plastic surgery to proctology, from orthopedics to ophthalmology and, as I previously mentioned, the specialty of family practice. There is an important difference among specialties, though. In some, such as internal medicine, a specialist must undergo an extensive reexamination periodically in order to remain board-certified. In others, the specialist must provide evidence to the board that he has attended a certain number of hours of continuing education in the specialty each year. In ob-gyn, neither of these is required, and a physician may, once board-certified, remain so for the rest of his life, even if he learns nothing further or forgets most of what he has learned, or if what he has learned has not prepared him to meet the real needs of his patients. For the rest of his career, the only people with an opportunity to evaluate his adequacy as a woman's doctor will be his patients.

The Private-Practice Environment

When an ob-gyn physician enters private practice he may be a solo practitioner, alone in his own office, or he may join a partner or a group. Regardless of how many other physicians share the physical office space, all ob-gyn specialists need several kinds of relationships, night-call swapping arrangements, referrals, and hospital privileges.

No matter how dedicated he may be, a specialist in ob-gyn cannot physically be available to respond to his patients' calls twenty-four hours a day, seven days a week, three hundred and sixty-five days a year. In order to survive he must arrange to swap on-call responsibility with one or more other physicians, so that he takes patient and hospital phone calls for the whole group when he is on duty, and he takes no calls when he is not. It may be every other night, every third, every fifth, or sometimes only for weekends, with weeknights not being swapped. The politics of this can be very intricate, since physicians with large practices may love taking calls for a new physician with few patients to bother them but may also be afraid that they will lose patients to a younger physician, especially if he is the one to respond to a middle-of-the-night call.

For obstetrical patients, it's critical that the doctors all go to the same hospital; otherwise the physician on call may find himself with one of his patients in labor at one hospital, and one of the other doctors' in labor at another. Other considerations include who accepts what kinds of payment, e.g., insurance, HMO, Medicaid, Medicare, and which hospital emergency rooms list the doctor on their call rosters.

Since most physicians don't know how to promote their own practices (having skipped all the business courses, psychology courses, and sociology courses in college, and having absolutely no notion of consumer satisfaction or customer relations), and established physicians have long made sure that advertising or competitive pricing remains socially unacceptable within medical circles, the new physician needs referrals from doctors in other specialties. Basically this works in simple ways: through the old-boy network, through the making of deals, and through the manipulation of power and influence.

Physicians court the older referral specialists (family medicine, internal medicine, pediatrics) who trained in the same medical center, went to the same college, or belong to the same clubs. They agree to refer patients to doctors who refer patients to them. They agree to give discounts to organizations that can direct patients to their office, such as HMOs, PPOs (Preferred Provider Organizations), Medicaid, and local self-insured businesses. Right away, the new physician has considerations other than the patient's welfare involved in his medical practice.

No ob-gyn physician can practice without a hospital where he can admit his patients. In order to do that, he has to apply for admission to the hospital staff, and when he does that he requests privileges to do specific types of procedures. Admission to a hospital staff is an automatic thing, as long as a doctor can prove he has passed all the landmarks described above—i.e., medical school, internship, and the obtaining of a license to practice medicine in that state. The hospital does not try to determine competence or quality or character except maybe to have the physician sign a statement that he has no mental aberration or drug addiction and has not lied on his application or hidden any pending legal action against him. Once admitted to the staff, each doctor has general hospital privileges; that is, he can admit patients and order the tests and procedures from which, along with daily room charges, the hospitals derive their profit.

If he wants to do obstetrics and gynecology, he must apply for specific privileges to do that. The credentials committee reviews the application form, and in addition to looking for the documentation of medical school, medical licensure, and internship, it looks for documentation of completion of an approved residency and the existence of malpractice insurance that covers ob-gyn. Sometimes a hospital will require that a staff ob-gyn observe the applicant physician in surgery and deliveries, for a time, to determine his competence. Almost no doctor welcomes this responsibility, and unless something truly catastrophic occurs the probationary period passes and the doctor is given full ob-gyn privileges. He will keep those privileges as long as he wants them, unless he commits some very severe atrocities indeed, and gets publicly caught at them.

Now he's in business, and the way he conducts himself will vary in many ways, but most commonly his primary motivating factor, whether he admits it or not, whether he is even conscious of it, will be money. It is an inescapable fact that money is what moves everything in our system of health care. The education of a doctor has taught him nothing about money, except how much of it he can expect to make. He will now set about to make sure that he makes at least that much, no matter what it takes.

Sixteen

CHOICES OF HEALTH-CARE PROVIDERS

ONE OF THE RESULTS OF OUR SYSTEM OF MEDICAL EDUCATION IS THAT ALL too often a patient's diagnosis is dictated by her choice of which type of specialist to see for the problem. Most American women choose a gynecologist as the source of their primary medical care. This results in a great deal of contact between women and gynecologists and, as I have discussed, the consequences of this contact can be unfortunate. The more times a woman consults a gynecologist the more likely she is to experience abuse.

There are a variety of medical specialists out there, and a variety of non-M.D. health-care providers. What each of us needs is a point of entry into the health-care system that acts to direct us in the right direction. What we need is a reliable source of *general* medical care. Lacking that, many women try to choose a specialist for each particular problem, and sometimes that choice, rather than the problem itself, dictates the diagnosis that is made. This can result in serious problems. Let me give you a factual example, then tell you about the choices of primary-care sources that are available to you.

Nina worked in the health-care arena, so she knew her options pretty well. As a medical-records clerk she had the opportunity to read the dictation of many physicians in many specialties, and her training made her familiar with the kinds of problems dealt with by each type of specialist. She didn't really have a primary-care physician. When she had a problem, she decided what kind of doctor to see for that particular need.

After she had given up on all the self-help remedies she had tried for her low-back pain, she decided to see an orthopedic surgeon. With her resources, it was easy to find one with a good reputation.

Nina was forty-two, a mother of two, divorced, and depressed. In addition to being lonely and bored she was increasingly forced into inactivity because of the pain she was experiencing. It wasn't there all the time, and she couldn't figure out what brought it on. Nothing seemed to make it better, though, at least nothing that she had tried.

Dr. Harris, the orthopedic surgeon, did all the usual things an orthopedist does to evaluate patients with back pain. This included an examination of her back and extremities, X rays, lab tests on her blood, and then, when all those were normal, a CT scan. This was also normal, so her physician was left with the usual diagnosis, "back strain." Nina was given medication to take and saw the physical therapist, who worked in Dr. Harris's office. He gave her a set of exercises and stretches to do and instructed her in how to properly stand, walk, sit, lift, and sleep.

Nina did all these things faithfully for a year, but her pain got worse. When she went back to Dr. Harris he repeated most of the tests, then told her that backs were mysterious things and that sometimes small injuries could cause severe pain. With nothing particular to be found on X ray or CT scan, there was no way to make a more specific diagnosis or to provide more effective treatment. He advised her to continue the medication and exercises and learn to live with her problem. He also pointed out that people tend to develop things like this as they get older.

Nina grew more depressed. Her life just wasn't much fun, and the idea that getting older would bring more problems like her back pain didn't make the situation any easier. During this time she began to have more trouble with her periods, and since she was due for a Pap smear, she referred herself to me.

In the course of reviewing her medical history I learned about her back pain. After questioning her for a while, it seemed to me that her pain was cyclic in nature, and that it got worse just before her periods. She had thought that she just noticed it more at that time because she always felt so awful right before her periods anyway, and her periods were so heavy and painful that she didn't do much during that time in her cycle.

When I examined her I found her uterus to be tilted back and essentially frozen in place. When I tried to move it at all she experienced extreme pain, not in her pelvis but in her back! In fact, the pain was identical to the back pain that she had experienced for years. It wasn't a tough diagnosis: Nina had endometriosis. A laparoscopy proved it and disclosed that it was very severe, involving both the tubes and the ovaries, which were stuck behind the uterus where most of the endometriosis had developed.

Because she was now forty-three, wanted no future pregnancies, and could be offered a "cure," rather than temporary relief, only by surgery, I did a hysterectomy, and was forced to remove both tubes and ovaries as well. This necessitated giving her replacement estrogen, which I was anxious to see the results of, as she had described having menopausal-type hot flashes prior to surgery. This suggested that her ovaries were no longer functional, perhaps having been completely destroyed by the endometriosis. The results were wonderful.

Nina was my patient for eight more years. In that time, not only did she not have any back pain but she had no hot flashes, lost weight, and started exercising and playing softball. She's happily married now and looks younger at fifty-one than she did when I first met her. As I've said, not every operation works out that well. In this case the endometriosis was only a contributing factor to her overall unhappiness. It was part of many things that combined to make Nina develop a dismal self-image. The endometriosis had given her pain, and the pain had caused a doctor to tell her that she was simply getting old and wearing out. The orthopedist had not only made the wrong diagnosis, he had compounded the harm with his lack of sensitivity.

It was a shame that it took so long for the diagnosis to be made, and it was a shame that she was treated for a nonexistent back problem for so long. But the situation illustrates well one of the hazards of seeing specialists: *Doctors tend to make diagnoses within their own specialty.* Specialists also tend to treat only the patient's specific complaint, almost never the whole patient. If you have back pain, for instance, the evaluation, and very likely the diagnosis, will depend on whether you first see a gynecologist, an internist, an orthopedist, or a neurologist. A good primary-care physician will approach any problem with enough competence, objectivity, and holism to get to the right answers and then get you to the right person or treatment. Besides gynecologists, then, who are the primary-care doctors for women, and how well do they fill the role?

Non-Gyn Primary-Care Physicians

A substantial number of women do not use a gynecologist for their primary care but instead rely on a family practitioner or an internist (internal-medicine specialist). If they are being treated by a specialist for some specific problem, they may even turn to their orthopedist, cardiologist, or general surgeon with all of their needs. There are potential problems with all of these choices, and other choices to consider as well.

FAMILY PRACTITIONERS

Family-practice physicians, whether specialty-trained in family medicine or not, attempt to meet all the needs of children and of men and women of all ages. While I admire the intent and believe that this area of medical practice tends to attract people more attuned to caring for the whole person, I feel that the needs of women (and of children, and of men, and of the elderly) are too complex to allow one physician to be very good, and very knowledgeable, in all of these areas. They do have some strong points as primary-care people for women, though, not the least of which is the fact that they generally don't do major surgery, including hysterectomies. It's clear that the more contacts that occur between women and gynecologists, the more uteruses are removed.

That's not the case with general practitioners, though I know one who has developed an interesting relationship with a gynecologist that leads to the same thing. This G.P. admits his female patients to the hospital for almost any abdominal complaint—pain, diarrhea, gas, menstrual cramps—then does a series of expensive procedures, always including a proctoscopy. He then calls in the gynecologist with the recommendation that a hysterectomy be done. The gynecologist has the G.P. assist at surgery, for which he collects an assistant's fee (20 percent of the surgeon's fee), and then the G.P. makes rounds each postoperative day and charges a consultation fee. All in all, he makes as much on the hospitalization as the gynecologist who performs the surgery. It's a variation on the old fee-splitting schemes, which are not prevalent anymore, but it illustrates one of the problems of the general practitioner. The greedy ones will find ways to overcome the fact that it's hard to make a lot of money unless you actually *do* something to a patient.

Surgical specialists have managed to command high fees for brief operations, but third-party payers (HMOs, insurance companies, and so on) don't reward well the long time good family practitioners spend in their offices, trying to meet the needs of the whole patient. They simply are underpaid for what they do, but they live in the same social realm as the surgical specialists, who may earn four or five times as much money, without ever being as generally valuable to the patients. They face the twin temptations of doing unindicated things to patients in order to increase income and of abandoning the effort to take the time required to meet the needs of the whole patient.

INTERNAL MEDICINE

Internists and other medicine specialists represent another primary-care issue. Their training has been such that they are knowledgeable about, and care about, the diagnosis and treatment of *disease.* There are exceptions, but the vast majority of them would prefer not to worry about promoting wellness, or dealing with the nondiseased person with needs of other kinds. Even if they knew how to diagnose and treat the common, minor illnesses special to women, such as menstrual abnormalities and vaginal infections, they would have little interest in doing so. In order to make the kind of living that they have come to expect, they must fill their days with patients who have serious illnesses, the treatment of which allows them to charge large fees. They have no high-ticket operations to fall back on.

Few of these physicians will have the necessary knowledge and skills to deal with such things as sexual or marital problems, and they neither understand nor care much about the fears that a woman has about her body, such as fears of breast cancer, fear that the spotting she experienced before her last period is the first sign of cancer, fears that menopause will bring the end of her attractiveness.

In this area, by the way, gynecologists can use their aura of authority to achieve something positive. Almost all women have these fears, and it was always my practice to anticipate them with particular patients, offer these patients solid information to allay unfounded fears, and give them appropriate screening tests and reassurance to replace unreasonable fears with a realistic picture.

Internists understand, and want to deal with, disease. If you have a disease, they are the people to see. But if you want help in being well, most are not going to meet your needs. If you want someone to understand all your concerns, and to value them as significant and worth attention, these specialists are likely to let you down.

Referrals

Getting referred to the right specialist when your primary-care physician suspects or determines that you need one is a process you should be knowledgeable about. If you have been fortunate enough to locate and establish the proper relationship with a good primary-care physician, you don't have to worry about being appropriately referred. This physician will only send you to a particular doctor if that doctor is the best one available for your problem, and will probably stay involved in your care, not for a fee but to be sure that you are getting treated well and that he or she feels secure about what is being done.

Many, many physicians make referrals for entirely different and inappropriate reasons. For instance, a gynecologist might have frequent occasion to refer a patient to a general surgeon, an internist, a cancer specialist (oncologist), or an orthopedist. The majority of such referrals are made not because the specific individual is the best available choice but perhaps because that person supports the same hospital, is an alumnus of the same training program, golfs with the gynecologist, belongs to the same country club, or has promised to refer a lot of patients to the gynecologist. These aren't necessarily bad reasons, but if the quality of the physician or the patient's experience with that physician is ignored, the patient is reduced to an item of financial or social exchange. This is another of so many areas where physicians' medical decisions are totally self-serving and have little to do with the welfare of the patient.

Alternatives to M.D.s

Assuming for a moment that the search for the right primary-care physician has been fruitless or is in process, a woman still needs help in understanding, preventing, or diagnosing the major threats to her well-being that are serious and constant issues for women today. These include breast cancer, cervical cancer, ovarian cancer, uterine cancer, and self-induced life-style problems, such as cigarette smoking, alcohol dependence, and less-than-ideal diet and exercise habits.

For effective screening tests and examinations and for a knowledgeable and compassionate ear, there are resources other than physicians that can often meet these needs as well or better than physicians. In fact, almost every need a woman has in the way of routine and preventive care can be met as effectively, but less expensively, by nonphysicians. Many HMOs have put that fact to good use, and it should be a major trend in health care, but it has been impeded by two things. First, as Paul Starr documented so well, American doctors have effectively worked to eliminate competition for health-care dollars, and for power, throughout our history. Second, the medical profession has managed to deceive many people with the inaccurate suggestion that any medical procedure not performed by an M.D. constitutes inferior care. This has resulted in patients' resistance to accept alternatives to M.D.s. Let me tell you about some of these professionals.

NURSE-PRACTITIONERS

Nurse-practitioners are nurses working in specialized roles as primary-care providers. They have received training in addition to that required for basic licensing as an R.N., and they have earned certification by the American Nurses Association. They become certified by first completing an ANA-certified training program, then passing a rigorous examination. They have advanced skills in assessing the physical and psychosocial health-illness status of individuals, families, and groups in a variety of settings, through health and development history-taking and physical examination.

In some instances, nurses specialize in a specific clinical area and have received certification in that specialty. Thus, there are family nurse-practitioners, pediatric nurse-practitioners, and ob-gyn nurse-practitioners.

You may find nurse-practitioners working with a physician in his or her office, or you may find them functioning independently in a nurse-staffed clinic, with overall supervision by a physician.

These specialized clinically trained nurses generally bring to their role the same kind of professionalism that tends to characterize nurses of all kinds. They take their training seriously, keep themselves up-to-date, and approach each patient and procedure with seriousness. When it comes to minor procedures like pelvic exams, Pap smears, diagnostic smears, and cultures, they tend to be more expert than physicians because they do not regard these things as trivial and they perform each one, each time, exactly as they were trained.

In the overall scheme of medical care, I believe that nurses are the professionals to be most respected. Their level of personal dedication is admirable, their training and continuing-education programs are top-notch, and their support systems for one another as managers, employees, and coworkers are consistently excellent. Unfortunately, nurses are the most abused professionals in America.

Nurses are overworked and underpaid, and their professional abilities are almost never fully utilized. Hospitals treat them like janitorial workers (though male janitors may get better pay), doctors treat them like servants, and yet they continue to strive for excellence in their work and to continually upgrade their skills. The opportunity for burnout is great, and capable men and women are pushed out of the nursing profession in large numbers by a combination of the stress of the work and the lack of reward for it. The result is that there are now about half as many nurses in this country as are needed.

The blame lies primarily with physicians. Physicians are mostly male, nurses are mostly female, and typical sex roles were imposed on the system long ago. Between the physicians' inappropriate level of authority and their arrogance, nurses simply haven't been utilized properly, or been given appropriate authority and respect. The only benefit from all this is that many good nurses try to achieve more professional autonomy by becoming nurse-practitioners, and you tend to find a very special group of women in these roles.

This caliber of professional woman may be found not only in gynecologists' offices but also in women's clinics and Planned Parenthood clinics. They are available for counseling, breast and pelvic exams, contraceptive advice, and help with referrals to other medical services. These kinds of facilities do a lot to fill some of the gaps left by the medical professional in meeting the needs of women.

Beware, however, the "Women's Centers" that are owned and operated by hospitals. They may also employ good people, but remember that the purpose of any program like this, which is developed and funded by a hospital, exists for one ultimate purpose: to refer patients to doctors on that hospital's staff and thus fill that hospital's beds. Their ads sound nice, but don't forget that hospitals are a business, and they survive (whether profit or nonprofit organizations) by having people occupy their beds, undergo tests, and receive treatment and surgery. For all of these things, they are absolutely dependent upon physicians.

144

OTHER NON-M.D. PROVIDERS

Besides nurses, there are other types of professionals who act as "physician-extenders." These include physician assistants, who are generally not nurses. Physician assistants have had their own training program specifically designed to prepare them to do routine screening, physical exams, and evaluation for physicians. All of the things I've said about nurses can be said for these people, and you should be comfortable seeing one of them in lieu of a physician. They will usually have more time to spend and will report their findings to the physician for whom they work before any decisions are made. Since you, or your HMO or insurance company, will be paying the physician for the visit, you have the right to demand to also see the physician, or to talk to him or her, if you wish.

PRIMARY CARE AFTER MENOPAUSE

Women who are postmenopausal and who have a reason (such as heart disease, diabetes, or arthritis) to be followed by a non-gyn specialist are better off staying away from gynecologists and trying to establish a satisfactory relationship with the specialist that is taking care of their major problem. Any major disease must be taken into consideration as part of any decisions about life-style, diet, or medications, so the physician responsible for managing a major illness has to be involved in the decisions concerning any and all health issues.

If these women are on estrogen-replacement therapy, though, they should be sure that their primary-care physician has the counsel of a gynecologist in managing that specific area. This is an area of considerable controversy and, increasingly, an area that requires specialized knowledge so that treatment choices can be made on an individual basis. (You can find more discussion of this in the last section.) Also, since during the postmenopausal years the develop-

145

ment of ovarian cancer is most likely, a regular pelvic exam by someone competent to do this well is advisable.

Summary

What every woman needs is a way of getting good primary care that will address all of her problems as well as her routine preventive care. She certainly needs to establish a primary-care physician who will be available to her in any situation that calls for urgent medical diagnosis and treatment. Either from this doctor or from one of the non-M.D. providers I have discussed, she also needs easy and comfortable access to the competent provision of a Pap smear, an annual mammogram, a routine pelvic exam, and a general physical at appropriate intervals, the frequency depending on her age and health. Preventive care should also include counseling, support, and information about health issues that are her own responsibility, including nutrition, exercise, stress management, and substance abuse.

The most important factor in the choice is that it should provide an effective point of entry for her into every area of medical care, should she need it. Ideally, women's health should be a primary-care specialty peopled by women professionals, and devoted to the primary and preventive health care of women. This could be a new specialty, or it could result from a transformation of the current specialty of ob-gyn. From a practical standpoint, it is more likely to develop from what now exists. For that to happen, however, the American College of Obstetrics and Gynecology must be forced to understand that the need exists, and it must decide to commit the specialty to becoming clearly a primary-care specialty. As it now stands, ob-gyn is a surgical specialty poorly equipped to provide primary medical care to women but unwilling to admit it. In managed-care systems like HMOs and PPOs, patients can refer themselves only to a primary-care physician, and access to specialty referral physicians is controlled by these primary-care "gatekeepers." Gynecologists want to have it both ways, even if it means that their patients are severely mistreated as a result.

Seventeen

OBSTETRICIANS AND MIDWIVES

THE VAST MAJORITY OF PREGNANCIES, LABORS, AND DELIVERIES ARE without major complication. Those that are complicated, of high risk, deserve the attention and effort of the best-trained board-certified obstetricians. Gigantic strides have been made in recent years in the ability of these physicians to bring about a happy conclusion to pregnancies that, if left alone, would end in tragedy. Major improvements have occurred in such areas as prematurity prevention and the management of pregnancies complicated by diabetes or other serious disease. Unfortunately, such increases in technology have not resulted in dramatic improvement in our best measures of the adequacy of maternity care, those being the maternal-mortality rate and the infant-mortality rate. The maternal-mortality rate stands at 8 maternal deaths for every 100,000 live births; that's two-and-a-half times the rate in Canada. The infant-mortality rate has, in fact, declined in recent years, to 10 in every 10,000 births; yet the United States is still twenty-second among modern nations in this regard.

In addition to scientific developments in obstetrics, there have been improvements at least as impressive in the technology used to help premature, low-birth-weight, and sick newborns survive. In my opinion this, not the changes in obstetrics, is the real reason for the slight improvement in neonatal survival in America.

To my knowledge, there are no studies which show that a lack of obstetricians results in a decrease in the successful outcomes of pregnancies. But there is good evidence that a lack of prenatal care results in a greater frequency of poor pregnancy outcomes. The prenatal care itself is the essential requirement, not the physician. Even though some types of technology can only be applied by M.D.s, their application of that technology does not necessarily bring about positive results. A good example of this is electronic fetal monitoring during labor. In a study by Dr. Al Haverkamp, published in 1979, it was shown that the use of fetal monitoring by physicians had resulted in an increase in delivery by C-section, but not an increase in infant survival. This study concluded that the increase in C-section had occurred because obstetricians had poorly interpreted the fetal-monitor record, and that if the obstetricians had not used fetal monitoring the extraneous C-sections would not have occurred. A technical bulletin published by the American College of Obstetrics and Gynecology, dated September 1989, states that currently available data support the conclusion that, during labor, listening intermittently to the fetal heart rate with a stethoscope is as effective as continuous electronic monitoring in detecting problems with the fetus.

Much has been said about the dramatic rise in the frequency of delivery of babies by cesarean section. It has been documented in medical journals, books, newspapers, and magazines and by the electronic media. In America, the frequency with which babies are delivered by cesarean section has quadrupled in the past twenty years, and it far exceeds the rate in other countries. The rate at which delivery by C-section occurs varies (from hospital to hospital) from almost none to over 60 percent of deliveries. The average in all hospitals is between one-fourth and one-third of all deliveries, and that rapidly growing number has been attributed to many things. Depending on who is explaining, or defending, the rate of

C-section, the list may include the increased use (or misuse) of electronic fetal monitoring, the rising rate of malpractice suits in obstetrics, or that obstetricians will earn in the neighborhood of 100 percent extra if a delivery is done by C-section. Some obstetricians even claim that it is the natural consequence of increasingly skillful obstetrics, a way to produce better pregnancy outcomes.

I can add little more in the way of statistics to the huge body of facts, figures, and opinions already published about this, but I think it is important to say that I firmly believe that the physician behavior element is the driving force behind the growth in the number of cesarean deliveries. Certainly there are situations in which a C-section is necessary for the life or well-being of the mother or baby. My personal opinion is that half or more of the C-sections done are unnecessary, and the procedure is performed for the wrong reasons.

One of the most common reasons, I believe, is simply that busy obstetricians are too impatient to wait through the prolonged labors that frequently occur if a policy of noninterference is maintained. Given a choice between, on the one hand, missing hours of sleep, skipping a leisure activity, or keeping an office schedule and, on the other, ending labor with a C-section while earning an extra thousand dollars or so, an obstetrician might find the situation becoming distorted in his mind. His altered perception makes it seem reasonable to opt for the C-section. Studies tell us that women who have had childbirth-education classes and women who are supported in labor by labor coaches or midwives have fewer C-sections. Apparently, these women don't let themselves be talked into C-sections as often. Women without prenatal training and those who don't have the objective advice and support of a sophisticated friend during labor are more easily manipulated.

Another common factor is that many obstetricians actually believe that by taking some kind of action they can always make things better, improve on what nature would produce if left alone. These obstetricians are too often found inducing labor, stripping membranes, rupturing membranes, prescribing a lot of medications, using forceps needlessly, and generally just interfering with the natural progression of things. Interference almost always creates more harm than good, but these doctors have come to feel that they are more wise, more skillful, and more infallible than they really are.

More harm than good is done by obstetricians who interfere with the course of a normal pregnancy, labor, or delivery. By this I mean not just unnecessary C-sections but interference in all sorts of ways where there is no indication for it except as a demonstration of the power and skill of the doctor. What I'm saying is that obstetricians taking care of uncomplicated, normal pregnancies may well pose a hazard to those pregnancies. Why is this the case, and why don't they leave otherwise unthreatened pregnant women alone?

The problem is that these physicians have, for economic reasons, maintained a system in which they are totally in control of obstetrical care, both routine and high-risk. They have prevented the development of a system that could produce not only quality obstetrical care from the standpoint of outcome, but also a more positive and need-fulfilling experience for pregnant women.

As things are most commonly done, a physician sees an obstetrical patient on an average of ten to fifteen times during a pregnancy. That's very good. The need for information and reassurance during pregnancy is great. A pregnant woman experiences fantastic physical changes as well as emotional turmoil while anticipating one of the most exciting, and frightening, events of her life. In fact, evidence has shown a positive correlation between frequency of prenatal visits and pregnancy outcome.

What is not good is that after a while many board-certified obstetricians are simply bored by routine pregnancies, with prenatal visits dominated by repetitive questions, instructions, and reassur-

151

ances. They often put all their obstetrical appointments in the same afternoon each week and allow something like five minutes per patient. The truth is that each of these patients represents around two thousand dollars of income, but few of them represent much of a medical challenge.

Physicians who are committed to meeting all of their patients' needs should feel that commitment as sufficient challenge and reward, but most do not.

The fact that a successful obstetrician will have an average of ten to twenty patients due each month means that he or she cannot be available, without personal or professional conflicts, for each patient's labor and delivery. In order to have some time to sleep, to see gynecological patients, to perform surgery, and for personal activities, virtually all obstetricians make arrangements with partners or colleagues to cover each other's practices on a regular, rotating basis. Though the patient goes through the pregnancy with the expectation that someone familiar will be available for the delivery and present for the labor, she often finds either a relative stranger standing in or her obstetrician present only sporadically.

The situation is so unsatisfactory for both patient and physician that it is amazing that it has not been changed. But obstetricians have resisted anything that would alter a system in which they receive large fees for every baby born, regardless of their degree of involvement or value in the process. This in spite of the fact that a staggering number of obstetricians get out of obstetrical practice each year due to the physically debilitating and relatively intellectually unrewarding nature of the activity and because of the growing frequency of malpractice suits. A more appropriate answer lies elsewhere, and it isn't new or untested.

Midwives

In countries where physicians do not enjoy the level of income, authority, or autonomy that physicians in the United States do, things are done differently. There midwives are responsible for all but the most high-risk and complicated pregnancies and deliveries, and obstetricians are called in for unforeseen complications of labor and delivery, or as consultants in high-risk pregnancies. The pregnant women in these countries not only enjoy a close, supportive relationship with a competent professional who often, during prenatal care, becomes a friend, but they experience better outcomes, in terms of lower perinatal infant mortality and a lower frequency of cesarean section.

But I don't need to cite European statistics to document my point, or the positive experience in Sweden or the Netherlands; there is evidence in America as well, old evidence and new.

In 1925, a White House conference on child health reported that the record of trained midwives surpassed the record of physicians in normal deliveries. This same conference concluded that the midwife took better care of her patients than did physicians because "she waits patiently and lets nature take its course." In 1930, a study by the New York Academy of Medicine reported that midwives had the lowest maternal-death rate of any birth attendant. The study concluded that physicians were responsible for 61 percent of the maternal deaths that occurred in the study group, while midwives were responsible for 2 percent, the rest not being attributable to an attendant.

I'm sure that obstetricians would argue that things have changed, but have they? In December 1989, an article appeared in the *New England Journal of Medicine* concerning the work of midwives, and it looked at the results obtained in birth centers. In these centers, 73 percent of which are run solely by midwives, pregnancy outcomes were as good as those of hospitals, though, not surprisingly, the C-section rates were dramatically lower.

In December 1986, the Congressional Office of Technology Assessment concluded that the quality of certified midwifery care was just as good as that provided by physicians, and they recommended that midwifery services should be expanded. In 1988, the National Commission to Prevent Infant Mortality recommended that state universities expand their training programs for certified nurse-midwives.

Perhaps you have experienced prenatal care from a midwife in your obstetrician's office and you're wondering why I seem to be suggesting that midwifery in America hardly exists. True, there are physicians who employ midwives, and the system is almost as good as an ideal system. Unfortunately, the obstetrical fees in those offices are just as high as in those without midwives. In these cases the obstetrician still collects the usual fee, while the midwife receives an unfairly low salary. Many hospitals (directed by their obstetrical departments) contribute to this by allowing only *certified nurse-midwives* to deliver babies, under direct supervision of obstetricians, and by restricting midwives who are not nurses from any involvement at all. This allows the obstetrician to maintain control of the fees. Further, if the obstetrician must be present for the delivery, as is the case in some hospitals, the motives come into play which cause unnecessary C-sections. In addition, the same relationships that exist between nurses of other kinds and doctors may exist in these relationships, and may impair the functioning of the nurse-midwives. Many states do not license nurse-midwives at all, and many more do not recognize midwives who are not nurses (these people prefer to be called direct-entry midwives).

Given that physicians are extraordinarily powerful in America compared to other countries, and understanding that obstetricians would lose a great deal of income if they gave up their control over maternity care, it is obvious why things are as they are in this country. The reasons are economic and have nothing to do with the provision of the best possible perinatal care.

I would like to see midwives assume the major role in the system of uncomplicated prenatal care, labor and delivery, and postpartum care, as well as prenatal education and postnatal education. Obstetricians should be available (those that so choose) to consult on, or manage, high-risk pregnancies, to manage high-risk labors, and to perform complicated deliveries. No one denies that obstetrical emergencies occur and that complicated pregnancies exist, and no one argues that the management of these things are what obstetricians are trained to do. When called upon to do so, they do it very well, but when managing a large volume of uncomplicated pregnancies, I believe, they do a great deal of harm. When they act as employers of midwives, they raise the cost of maternity care and divert income from the people who deserve it.

I would have midwives function either as stand-alone professionals or as the professional staff of hospital birthing facilities or birth centers. The total fee would be composed only of the institution's fee and the midwife's fee, and obstetricians would be paid only when needed in consultation.

There should be, as there should be in all of health care, competition for the consultation, so that fees could arrive at the lowest open-market price.

What Happens to the Obstetricians?

Even though I would like to see obstetricians disappear as the primary providers of uncomplicated obstetrical care, I do not advocate the removal of the ob-gyn specialist as the top candidate for development into a primary-care specialist for women. It may seem, at this point, that I have tried to put women in such fear of gynecologists that they will begin to march on offices and clinics with torches and wooden stakes.

Please understand that I have not intended to say that there are no gynecologists capable of meeting the needs of their patients. Nor do I mean to imply that only a gynecologist might have the right combination of skills to be a good primary-care physician for women. I do mean that, for a start, gynecologists come closer than anyone to having the basic knowledge that prepares them for meeting all the needs of women. What they need, in order to become something worthwhile, is for the health-care system to be changed so that inappropriate and harmful rewards are removed; for women as a group to make gynecologists understand their needs and expectations; and for women to assume leadership in the specialty of obstetrics and gynecology. Male gynecologists need to undergo a process of attitude adjustment and to be reeducated and reoriented toward an appropriate level of understanding, regard, and respect for women. Accomplishing all of this certainly won't be easy, but it is sometimes surprisingly simple to change at least the behavior of physicians.

When I moved to Colorado Springs in 1974 to begin my practice, I found that only one of the hospitals here allowed fathers in the delivery rooms to watch the birth of their children. The physicians in the other hospitals thought the fathers would at best be a nuisance and at worst misinterpret things they saw and file lawsuits. I convinced my older partners to join me and the other younger partners in attending one meeting of the obstetrical section of that hospital (which they had stopped attending, because they no longer did obstetrics). They agreed to support our argument for a family-centered birth experience, and we simply outnumbered the relenting skeptics.

To this day, I don't think the physicians who practiced in that hospital would have made a change unless forced. Since then, consumer pressure and competition have made them go on to add birthing rooms, prenatal education, and father-assisted deliveries and to allow labor coaches. This kind of pressure must be applied in all areas of women's health care.

In the next chapter I will try to describe the appropriate relationship that should exist between a woman and her primary-care physician, how to look for a primary-care physician, how to relate to him or her, and what to expect from the resulting interaction. The things I say should apply to any primary-care physician and, in part, to any physician at all.

Eighteen

LOOKING FOR DOCTOR RIGHT

IT IS SELF-EVIDENT THAT THERE IS A GAP BETWEEN THE NEEDS WOMEN bring to their gynecologist and the experience they take away. I hope I have shown that the size of that gap is much greater than has been evident to women not "privileged" to be inside the health-care system.

Most women will agree on the desired characteristics of the primary-care physician that we might call Dr. Right. Dr. Right should first be competent, and as knowledgeable as any other physician in the specialty. It is desirable that such a doctor be good with their hands, gentle, effective, and talented in the operating room as well as the examination room. Of equal importance would be sensitivity, compassion, honesty, empathy, and genuine caring, not for money or ego-massaging but for women, individually and collectively.

Certainly, those characteristics constitute the "right stuff," but they will not result in Dr. Right being able to meet all your needs unless the relationship is right. I hope that you by now agree that the best chance you have to find a gynecologist with most of the right stuff is if *he* is a *she*. Unfortunately, there simply are not enough female doctors to go around. As of this writing, women constitute approximately 25 percent of the Fellows of the American College of Obstetrics and Gynecology. I would like to offer some suggestions as to how you can help bring about the rise of women to leadership in the ob-gyn specialty, then talk about the search for Dr. Right among the physicians, mostly male, that now occupy the position.

You can begin by expressing your preference for seeing a woman for your care whenever the option is available to you. If a woman gynecologist is not available or her practice is full, find a gynecologist who has a female nurse-practitioner working in his office and ask to see her for your routine exams. If women consistently send the message that they are serious about their preference for women it will encourage female physicians to specialize in ob-gyn. It will also let male gynecologists know that something is wrong with their performance, a threat that usually gets the attention of men.

To underscore that message, there should be a call for action from every feminist organization in the country, on several fronts. These groups should demand that gynecologists be educated, at every opportunity, about the problems that exist for women, the needs that are not being met, women's intolerance for continued abuse, and the necessity for males who want to be physicians for women to reexamine themselves as males and redefine themselves and their approach to their patients. Gynecologists attend an incredible number of continuing-education meetings, and this issue could be made part of every one of them, ideally taught by women. If, for instance, the American College of Obstetrics and Gynecology were to mount a joint effort with the National Organization for Women, the resulting reeducation of gynecologists could result in dramatic improvement in a relatively short time.

Failing that kind of cooperative effort, each woman should deliver the message to her own physician, by giving him feedback concerning the areas in which her needs are not being met, by him or by his practice environment.

The public discussion about sexual harassment in the workplace that followed the Clarence Thomas Supreme Court hearings made two facts very clear. First, that a great deal of sexual harassment occurs, and second, that much of it is not reported. I have to wonder whether a great deal of sexual harassment and abuse occurs in doctors' offices that also doesn't get reported. It is easy to imagine that a woman who has been inappropriately fondled or subjected to unwanted sexual advances by a doctor might leave his office doubting her own perspective of the incident. She might wonder whether she really experienced what she thought she did, or if she just misinterpreted the behavior. It is easy to imagine that she might feel too embarrassed about the incident to talk to anyone about it, and it is understandable that she would feel powerless to do anything about it in any case. It is especially easy for me to believe that such things occur in gynecologists' offices because I have had many encounters of that kind described to me by patients and friends.

It is vitally important that such things be reported, and there is a way to do it. Obviously, a gross sexual assault should be reported to the police. But if you have been sexually harassed or abused by a doctor in more subtle ways you should write to the grievance committee of the State Board of Medical Examiners. Describe exactly what occurred and demand that you be told what action will be taken. Perhaps a single reported episode will not result in effective action, but repeated allegations concerning the same physician will not be ignored. You should send the same sort of report concerning any other complaint you have about your treatment by a doctor. In Colorado, the Board of Medical Examiners responds to letters that complain about the conduct of a physician by first notifying the physician, in writing, of the nature of the complaint. He has twenty days to reply, though he has no legal obligation to do so. After his reply is received, or twenty days passes, an investigation is carried out. In 1989–90, the Colorado Board received 592 complaints and took some disciplinary action in 59 cases. Six doctors had their licenses suspended. I assume that a similar process is used in other states as well, so there is a viable mechanism for you to make something happen.

Needless to say, it is better to avoid abuse by being well informed about specific doctors. Both individually and through their organizations, women need to go on record as demanding the release of information about gynecologists (indeed, all doctors) that is now withheld from them. This information should include an individual physician's education, certifications, record of complaints filed with the State Board of Medical Examiners, hospital data on such things as C-section rates, surgical and obstetrical complication rates, and depth of experience with various procedures and technologies. If every woman simply had access to the actual track record of physicians the first stage of looking for Dr. Right would be a lot easier.

Until all of these things are accomplished, you have to deal with the available choices. Before thinking about *whom* it is that you are looking for, it is important for you to know *what* you are looking for. What kind of relationship with a gynecologist is going to produce the best outcome from your medical encounters?

I would like to suggest that the appropriate relationship between a woman and her gynecologist is that of intimate friends. Before you respond to the word "intimate," let me elaborate, because I use the word in its proper meaning rather than its common usage.

Real intimacy exists in a relationship when you are able to expose yourself completely—physically, intellectually, and emotionally, without fear of judgment, rejection, or abuse, and with the secure expectation of acceptance. It is something we all need in our lives, with a spouse, a friend, or family. Women are especially talented at establishing intimate relationships with other women, but most do not expect this kind of relationship with their doctor and don't try for it, leaving the doctor on a pedestal, or at least on some unreachable plane of social existence.

It is common for women to say that they could not go to a friend for their gynecological care. Why not? What could be more comfortable than to be examined by, or seek advice from, a genuine friend who cares about you, and accepts, without judgment or abuse, whatever you are. Perhaps the problem is the definition of "friend." I wouldn't suggest that the doctor you should see is the acquaintance you watch making passes at others' wives, or at you, at the country club each weekend. I would suggest that anyone you know well, and respect in the areas of his or her life that you observe, may be someone to whom you could intimately relate in a medical setting.

What you are ideally seeking is intimacy. Not sexual intimacy, but the intimacy of a real friend, which does involve the same kind of trust and acceptance that you and your spouse or partner, I would hope, also share.

There is, of course, no place for seductiveness or sexual exploitation of any kind in a medical relationship. The doctor that flirts with you, or even jokes about his awareness of your sexual attractiveness, is absolutely out of line. But there is a great difference between seductiveness and familiarity. You want to have a doctor who is familiar with your body in the same way that you are. Someone who can comfortably discuss anything about your body, or your sexuality, while making you feel that you are talking to a close friend.

Whatever your appearance, your body has an objective reality that needs appropriate scrutiny by a physician. You need to be able to take your body, regardless of its size, shape, or age, to a medical person who accepts it only as the vehicle that carries the person, and who relates to it, and to you, as both a competent professional and a caring, accepting friend. If you have difficulty in accepting your body yourself, it won't make it easier if you see a doctor who accentuates your self-consciousness.

Considerations about exposing yourself physically should be a small and a relatively unimportant part of appropriate expectations from a doctor as an intimate friend. You should be able to expose your feelings and your fears, discuss your relationships, your sexuality, your sexual activities, or your desires, and ask any questions with the absolute certainty that you will not be judged and that you will not be treated differently because of what you have revealed. You should be able to totally dismiss any concern that your confidence will be betrayed, not because the AMA code of ethics denounces it but because you are relating to a friend with whom you have a trusting, intimate relationship.

As a practicing gynecologist, I especially valued, and will always remember, the patients who treated me like a real human being and like a friend. Unfortunately, though I tried to create an atmosphere that encouraged it, many patients did not respond to the opportunity. In retrospect, I have decided that they simply didn't know that it was acceptable, because the overwhelming picture of the physician-patient relationship, one which doctors have created, is of an authoritative, not-to-be-questioned, powerful doctor and a dependent, passive, not-as-important-as-the-doctor patient. I obviously failed to consistently avoid this stereotype. Such a relationship is not only counterproductive, it is one that women do not have to accept. Women have the power to change this dramatically, as individuals with their own physicians and as a powerful consumer group addressing the entire system of health care. As an individual, once you have defined the relationship that you want, you will be ready to find the individual with whom you want to create it.

Begin with credentials. Doctors will consider this heresy, but it's not all that hard to be a well-trained physician with good credentials, and there is no reason to settle for less. You can start by calling the medical society in your county and asking for a list of board-certified gynecologists (or internists, or family-medicine specialists, etc.). At your library there are directories, such as the *Directory of Medical Specialists,* that can tell you when and where these doctors received their training and when they received their board certification. Although you will not be able to determine the practice experience, complications, or C-section rates of an individual physician, you can often determine, by calling the hospital, what the C-section rate is for that hospital. It is mandated that the information be made available in many states, but hospitals will often tell you if asked. If you know that the doctor you are interested in seeing is one of the only group that delivers babies there, you will have a lot of information. If there are many groups of doctors that contributed to the data about that hospital, it won't mean as much, but when you ask the physician to tell you what his individual rate has been, you will have figures with which to compare, and if he says his rate is lower you have a good opportunity to explore what it might be about his practices that have brought it about.

Lists of doctors that are provided by hospitals, or other organizations with self-serving interests, will not be complete; in fact, they will only list the doctors they are trying to promote. If you ask a hospital for referral to an obstetrician, for instance, be aware that their list will not reflect the entire community, but only the doctors that admit to their hospital.

If you have trusted friends who can relate their experiences with given doctors, by all means listen. But don't accept statements like "He's O.K." Ask for details of the friend's experience with the doctor, his office, and his partners. Try to find out if your friend has had a good experience, or if it has just been marginally acceptable. If you have access to a nurse who works in an operating room or the gyn floor of a hospital, talk to her. She probably knows more about the character and competence of the physicians than anyone you are likely to find. Beware the nurse who works *for* a doctor, though. I have personally experienced the wrath of doctors whose control or income I've threatened, and their employees are vulnerable.

If you personally know a gynecologist socially, you have an opportunity for valued input. If you don't like the way he behaves in social situations, if you don't find yourself able to have a reasonably open conversation with him, or if he clearly stereotypes women, you will not get along with him as your physician. Remember, you're trying to find someone with whom you can build a truly intimate relationship.

If you know a physician in some other, non-gyn specialty well enough to trust him or her to be entirely honest with you, ask about the gynecologists in town. Most doctors know who's who, and they will know, especially, which gynecologists have the reputation for doing too many operations, creating too many complications, or lacking discretion in talking about their patients. They also know who the rip-off artists are, in terms of billing and unnecessary procedures designed to generate income. This doctor will have to be a very good friend and an extraordinary person to admit it to you though, as most doctors won't consciously admit it to themselves.

If the company where you work is large enough to be self-insured, sometimes the person in charge of personnel benefits will have data and experience with the billing practices of the town's gynecologists, and that person can tell you which ones are abusers.

* * *

Once you have picked a doctor to try you must see him with an open mind. Don't try to quickly make him acceptable; try to determine whether he really is. The first-visit experience is revealing. If the receptionist or the nurse is rude, or if your waiting time is excessive, there is always the possibility that it was an unusual event. But if you question the doctor about it and he either doesn't care or gets angry at you, leave, and try someone else.

With you as a brand-new patient, the doctor should provide the time and make the effort to make you comfortable and to get to know you, medically and personally. Meeting you for the first time *after* you have undressed shows a lack of sensitivity that probably will be reflected in everything else he does.

Should the nurse ask you to undress and wait for the doctor, request that you be allowed to talk with him with your clothes on first. If she or the doctor refuses or gets angry, leave. Anything that puts you on an unequal footing with the doctor is inappropriate. There is no reason for you to undress for a complete stranger, which that doctor will be until you have had a chance to meet and talk. You probably dressed yourself nicely to meet this new person, who may become a close friend, and it is demeaning to have you present yourself, for your first encounter, naked and thus already in a vulnerable role.

Names may be important, too. If he insists that he is *Doctor* So-and-So and you are Judy, or Dear, or Hon, something is wrong with his sense of things. Let him know what you prefer to be called. If you would like to call him by his first name and he is offended by that but wants to call you by your first name, something is wrong with him.

At your first meeting try to accomplish two things: letting the doctor know who you are and what your expectations are from a doctor, and finding out about his attitudes, methods, personal style with patients, and expectations from you.

You should determine whether he is genuinely willing to be a primary-care physician and have you come to him with all your needs. You should also determine how he will communicate with you in the future, how phone calls will be answered, how you would get to see him in an emergency or for an acute problem needing a same-day appointment, and who covers his practice when he is not on call at night or is on vacation. Even though the specific answers to these questions may be important to you, it is more important that he is comfortable with your asking them and is willing to take the time to discuss it. It will take some time to learn how really sensitive and responsive he is, but you might test him a little on the first visit. Ask questions and express any concerns you might have about any aspect of your body. You want to see how he relates as much as what he says. The important thing is getting a reassuring, honest, and concerned response, and the sense that you have met a physician whom you would choose to see again.

If the first visit is like so many women's experiences, humiliating, demeaning, frustrating, infuriating, or simply disappointing, try someone else. It may take years to find the right doctor, but it also may be years before you need one so badly right away that it is worth accepting insensitive treatment. If the first visit goes well and is encouraging to you, then you can begin to slowly shape the relationship into what you are seeking: an intimate friendship with a competent professional. (I'm well aware that intimate relationships are not easily or quickly created, but the goal is worthwhile, and the effort itself may bring better results than you have ever had.)

A woman has to engage the gynecologist in the same way that she would any person whom she wished to treat her well or whom she wanted to be at ease with her. You must bring *yourself* to the interaction; you must present yourself and your needs to the gynecologist, so that he can respond to *that person* and *those needs,* and not to some generic patient. To do this takes some personal courage and some self-assurance, but it is critical that you become a real person to the doctor. It is also critical that you treat the doctor like a real person. He is half of this intimate relationship, and his needs cannot be ignored. You cannot expect to have him care a great deal about you and know all about you if you know nothing, and care nothing, about him.

Some days he too may be sick, or depressed, or exhausted, or frustrated, and there is no reason why you cannot express concern and support, or at least sensitivity, to these things. A friendship in which one party is always needful, the other always helpful will not long be sustained. The right relationship will not develop if you insist on being only a passive user of services.

The relationship you are trying to build will take some time, even with good intentions on both sides. But it is important to remember that this doesn't mean total, blind acceptance. You are not trying to simply accept whatever is offered, you are trying to create an appropriate relationship, so you must demand that it be appropriate.

Don't give your trust until it is earned, and don't accept insensitive treatment, demeaning procedures, or lack of personal regard. Women have, in some measure, helped create the bad practices that exist by accepting them. The practices are not unchangeable, and all women must begin to do more than just express dissatisfaction. They must cease to reward bad behavior. If you explain to your doctor that his attitude, or habits, or office systems are humiliating to you, and if he does not respond appropriately and change things, leave him and tell him why you left.

* * *

To whatever degree you cannot effect change by finding genuine caring in physicians, you can depend on greed to be an effective motivator. If women can effectively act in concert to reward only appropriate behavior from gynecologists, the change will be remarkable. This means getting involved with the ways that doctors are paid, as well as how many patients they have.

Insurance companies, HMOs, PPOs, and large self-insured businesses are all trying hard to gain some control over medical expenses. The harder they try to pay physicians appropriate fees, only for things that are necessary, and only when the physician actually performs the service, the harder the physicians work to maintain the opportunity to control fees, manipulate charges, and perform unnecessary procedures without being challenged.

As long as I can remember, patients have allied themselves with physicians, against the third-party payers, by asking doctors to manipulate diagnoses so that what might not have been covered is paid for by these insurers. They have also maintained the attitude that it's the insurance company's money being lost when doctors charge inappropriately, so they haven't bothered to become involved. The result has been steadily increasing insurance premiums. More important, this attitude has allowed physicians to maintain control of their incomes, without being accountable to anyone for the quality of their services.

Remember that no matter how you are insured, ultimately it is you who pays the doctors' bills, and thus it is ultimately you who has to provide appropriate feedback about the service you are given. Women should refuse to pay for shabby treatment. They should provide information to their insurance company or HMO concerning lack of quality and service. They should let them know when their doctor has submitted a bill that is inappropriate for what was done (for instance, a bill for a complete new-patient exam when they in fact had a ten-minute visit for a vaginal infection).

As I said earlier, you have to let a doctor know if he is not meeting your needs, and if you decide to change physicians, let him know that you are seeking elsewhere what he is failing to provide. There is no more reason to provide income for a bad doctor than to pay for rotten apples at the market. A great deal has been accomplished in our country by aggressive consumerism, and the medical profession can be made responsive to its consumers in the same fashion.

In a system dominated by greed and arrogance there are, in fact, many good people practicing medicine, with good and proper motivation. It is possible to restore the time when these were in the majority and greed was a rare result of the power and authority derived from a medical degree. It is time to stop rewarding anything that hints of shabby treatment or lack of regard for women, and to begin to reinforce everything that approximates what is so often claimed and so seldom experienced—genuine caring for women.

SECTION FOUR

Information
and Advice

INTRODUCTION

THIS SECTION HAS TWO PURPOSES: TO GIVE YOU INFORMATION ABOUT THE
most common gynecological problems women experience and to
advise you about how to relate to a physician with regard to those
problems.

You can use it as a basic textbook if you are interested in
becoming better informed about gynecological problems in general,
or you can use it as a reference about particular problems.

In each area I have tried to give you an overview of the things
you and your physician should be considering when faced with a
problem of that type. Then I have listed the questions that you
should be prepared to ask in order to really understand your alternatives.

Most of us think of appropriate questions to ask after we have
left a doctor's office. If you know what you are dealing with before
your appointment, take the questions with you. If you can't be
prepared in advance, make a follow-up appointment and refer to
this section prior to that visit. It is a bad idea to be diagnosed and
agree to surgery at the same visit.

In the past decade, much has been said about second opinions,
especially with regard to surgery. Unfortunately, studies have
shown that second opinions have very little value. Doctors rarely
admit to patients that a physician in their own community has given

bad advice. Rather than seeking a second opinion regarding your diagnosis or treatment, I would suggest that you seek a series of first opinions. Go to one or two different physicians as though you are a new patient. Present your problem, and do not reveal that you have already received a recommendation. If you can get fresh opinions from say, three physicians, it will usually be clear to you whether there is a clear consensus about your options. There is also value in the comparison among the physicians and their manner of dealing with you.

Nineteen

WHEN A HYSTERECTOMY?

TO UNDERSTAND THE EFFECTS OF A HYSTERECTOMY, YOU MUST understand what a uterus does and doesn't do. The uterus is basically a muscle, the size of a pear, with a specialized lining of its inner cavity that responds to hormones produced by the ovaries. The uterus goes through a monthly cycle designed to do one thing: receive a fertilized egg and support the developing fetus if pregnancy occurs. If pregnancy does not occur, the lining sloughs off with the menstrual bleeding, and the process starts over again. The uterus does not make any of the female hormones, and, even though it is involved in sexual response and orgasm, it is not necessary for sexual response and orgasm.

There is a great deal of confusion about terminology. The word *hysterectomy* comes from the Greek *hyster* (womb) and *ecto* (out); together they mean "to remove the uterus." Many years ago it was common to remove only the upper portion of the uterus and to leave the cervix, or lower portion, in place. It was thus necessary to distinguish a total hysterectomy from a partial hysterectomy. But for some reason, people began to think that a total hysterectomy meant removal of the uterus, fallopian tubes, and ovaries. Physicians use the term *total hysterectomy* to indicate removal of the entire uterus; another term, *salpingo-oophorectomy,* indicates removal of the tubes and ovaries.

175

There are two ways to remove the uterus: through an incision in the abdomen or through the vagina. The decision as to which approach to take is fairly simple, but the simplicity escapes many gynecologists. A hysterectomy should be done through the vagina when it's easy to do that way, when there is no risk that other structures are abnormally adhered to the uterus (the intestine, for instance), and when the uterus is not too large to prevent the physician from safely performing the surgery vaginally. The procedure should be done through the abdomen whenever it is too difficult and risky to do vaginally, or when there is a need to get a good look at the other structures inside the abdomen.

I have known older gynecologists who had simply grown tired of the increased effort required to do a vaginal hysterectomy. These gynecologists did them all abdominally, and so subjected many patients to a needless scar and to potential aftereffects of abdominal surgery.

I have also known gynecologists who felt it a macho challenge to take out any uterus through the vagina, even when the risk to the patient was clearly greater. These tended to be the same doctors who took great pride in doing their surgery faster than anyone else, and persisted in trying to set personal speed records, in spite of the fact that they tended to have surgical-complication rates higher than anyone else. A look at the statistics shows clearly that as speed increases beyond the average, complication rates go up.

The truth is, I have known gynecologists whose surgical skills were so minimal that they *consistently* had high complication rates, but I have never seen one refer a patient to a more skillful surgeon because the case was going to be especially difficult and deserved the best surgeon available (except for a few cases where the patient had no ability to pay for the surgery).

All of these doctors could be identified for you by operating-room nurses, the ones who watch these doctors operate every day, if only you could have free access to them. As a group, operating-room nurses have always impressed me with their professionalism as well as with their ability to understand all their surgeons' strong and weak points and to do their best to compensate for them. It would be interesting to see what would result if they were given the responsibility of awarding or revoking hospital-surgical privileges.

Doctors who do a lot of hysterectomies like to say that the uterus bleeds, cramps, has babies, and gets cancer, and if you don't value any of these things you should obviously have it removed. Sounds good, doesn't it, so why not?

Complications of Hysterectomy

There are good reasons why not to have an unnecessary hysterectomy, not the least of which is that you might die from a complication of the operation. This could happen from a number of causes, even when the procedure is performed competently. Blood clots can form in the veins of the pelvis or the legs, break free, and go to the lungs, causing sudden death in an otherwise asymptomatic postoperative patient. You can begin to hemorrhage postoperatively and die before you can be taken back to the operating room and get the bleeding stopped. You can develop an infection that fails to respond to antibiotics and results in death. You can die as a result of an anesthetic complication or mistake. You can die from a reaction to medication, or from administration of the wrong medication.

Short of death, there are other possible complications that are not worth risking. There can develop, from surgical error, an abnormal connection between the rectum and the vagina, called a recto-vaginal fistula, which results in the passage of feces into the vagina. The repair of this problem is difficult and, at worst, may never be successfully accomplished or may require a colostomy for months before the repair can be done. Also as a result of surgical error, the ureter (the tube that carries urine from the kidney to the bladder) may be tied off, and if this is not immediately recognized and repaired it can cause the loss of a kidney. Less severe, but still fairly undesirable complications include infections involving the ovaries, incisional infections, ovaries that adhere to the top of the vagina and cause pain with intercourse . . . the list goes on.

It is fair to say that these things are not common results of hysterectomy. The death rate from all hysterectomies is about 1 out of each 1,200 done. But if only *one* patient dies as a complication of an operation that did not need to be done, isn't that too many?

I've always wondered how many hysterectomies done for less than absolutely sound indications would have been done if each patient had been straightforwardly told all the possible outcomes, so that she really understood them and believed that they could happen to her. I have heard many a surgeon say, "If I did *that* [tell the patient everything], I'd *never* do any surgery."

Indications for Hysterectomy

So when should a hysterectomy be done, and what are the effects? Simply stated, it should be done when there is no reasonable alternative and the benefits outweigh the risk of complication. Specifically, there are four indications for removal of the uterus:

1. Cancer of the uterus, tubes, or ovaries.
2. Menstrual bleeding so heavy as to cause anemia that cannot be controlled by taking iron, and which has failed to respond to all possible treatment alternatives. (There are more good treatments being developed, which I will describe in Chapter Twenty-eight.)
3. Benign tumors of the uterus so large that they threaten to block the ureters, cause severe pain or uncontrollable bleeding, and absolutely cannot be treated with medication

or removed while leaving the uterus intact. (These alternatives are discussed in Chapter Twenty-two.)

4. Chronic pelvic inflammatory disease that causes intolerable pain and is absolutely not surgically treatable with techniques short of hysterectomy.

Any other situation requires that you get some specific answers to a few questions, weigh the risk versus the benefit, and decide for yourself. DON'T LET PHYSICIANS DECIDE FOR YOU. It's your body, not theirs, and you'll live with the consequences of the surgery for the rest of your life. Their motivation for choosing one alternative over another may be monetary, and with more and more alternatives available you need to be armed with enough information to make the decision yourself. What you need to know to make a good decision is straightforward:

A. You should know exactly what is wrong with you and what all the possible treatment approaches are.

B. You should know the possible consequences of doing nothing. You should know the possible complications of all possible treatments, including hysterectomy.

C. Last, you should know all the effects that any of the treatments, including hysterectomy, might have on you.

If, in the end, you either must have surgery or you choose to trade the risks for the benefit, there is some good news. Removal of the uterus, barring complications, has no serious bad effects. You will have no more menstrual periods. Even though your hormonal cycles continue normally, controlled by the ovaries, there is no uterine lining present to respond and bleed. You will have no risk of pregnancy, and no need for birth-control measures. You will have no risk of developing uterine or cervical cancer. You will be able to take estrogen at menopause without the concern that it will increase your risk of uterine cancer.

Removal of the uterus alone will not, barring complications, cause any change in your production of any hormone, or cause an early menopause.

The Question of Removing the Ovaries

If you agree to have your uterus removed, you may be asked to decide if you want to, or may be told that you must, have your ovaries removed as well. Many gynecologists routinely recommend that this be done if you are close to menopause, with the rationale that at menopause the ovaries are of no use to you and yet are still subject to the development of cancer. This sounds like a good argument, but one wonders if the same attitude would apply if the gynecologist's testicles were the organs in question.

At menopause, the ovaries cease to function and no longer produce estrogen. The cessation of estrogen production is responsible for experiences such as hot flashes, decreased vaginal moisture, and, sometimes, mood swings. The average age at which menopause occurs is fifty. That's the average; it begins later in some women. In spite of this, your gynecologist might suggest removal of the ovaries along with the hysterectomy as early as age forty. Don't do it! Don't ever let anyone convince you that removing normal tissue is a reasonable thing to do. The only exception is in women with a family history of ovarian cancer. In these women, there is a strong case for removal of the ovaries solely to eliminate the risk of cancer. This is so because for a woman whose mother or sister has developed the disease, the odds of getting it herself are high. Because early detection is the only way to produce a reasonable chance of a cure, and early detection of ovarian cancer is not very likely, any woman with a family member who has had this kind of cancer *must* see a gynecologic cancer specialist and discuss her alternatives.

After menopause the ovaries have no function, and no harm is done by removing them. That would still not be a reason to take them out, except for the fact that some of them are destined to develop cancer, even in women without a family history. Thus if you are to have a hysterectomy and you are already past menopause, it is reasonable to remove the ovaries. This would not be true if removal would add complication or risk to the surgery.

The important thing to remember is that if you are not already menopausal removal of the ovaries will produce menopause, just like the menopause that will occur naturally someday. If you don't want that to happen and there is no necessity for removing the ovaries, don't be talked into it. I'll talk more about menopause in Chapter Twenty-nine.

Twenty

POSTOPERATIVE COMPLICATIONS

WHATEVER TYPE OF SURGERY YOU MAY HAVE, ONCE THE ACTUAL procedure is done there is a time of healing, then gradual resumption of normal feelings and activities. There is always discomfort, and there is always fatigue, for some time after surgery. In addition, specific operations produce specific postoperative symptoms. You will normally experience anxiety before and after surgery, so it is important that you know ahead of time what to expect, what is normal and what is not. Here's how to prepare yourself to deal with the postoperative experience and to be ready to identify complications if they develop:

1. Before surgery, ask your doctor what to expect following the operation, day by day, and write it down. Find out when you are expected to be perfectly normal again. Be sure to note the negative things you will *normally* experience.

2. After surgery, compare your experience with your notes. If anything deviates significantly in terms of pain, fever, bleeding, wound healing, energy level, or other things, ask for an explanation. Your doctor should be able to tell you not only what is wrong but what will be done about it and how long it should take for it to resolve.

182

3. If it does not resolve in that time, or if your doctor cannot convince you that the situation is well in hand, ask for a consultant to be called in to see you. If you are already out of the hospital, you should call one yourself. (In the hospital a good source of advice about whom to call would be one of the R.N.s on the gyn unit. In fact, if there is one you particularly like write down her name and the phone number on the gyn floor before you go home.)

Don't forget my previous advice about surgery. Obtain a copy of the doctor's operative summary and a copy of the pathology report and take it to another doctor after surgery. Ask for an objective opinion about the necessity for your surgery, in the light of the findings at the time of operation. Also ask about the appropriateness of the particular surgical approach that was used.

The best way to obtain these documents is to have had your doctor agree to provide them to you before the operation. If your doctor balks at giving them to you, go to another doctor and have him or her request them. If this doesn't work, an attorney can get them for you.

None of this should pose a problem if you are dealing with an honest, well-meaning physician, but you should be aware that the rise in malpractice suits and awards has made the entire health-care system quite nervous about disclosing information. Malpractice-insurance carriers have instructed doctors to notify them if an attorney asks for records.

Remember that while the original copy of the patient's records may belong to the physician or the hospital, the *information* belongs to the patient. No one has the right to withhold this from you.

Twenty-one

PAP SMEARS

MOST WOMEN WHO REGULARLY SEE A GYNECOLOGIST TIME THEIR VISIT around an annual Pap smear. Named for Dr. Papanicolaou, who invented it, the Pap smear is one of the most effective screening techniques for cancer ever developed. Unfortunately, it often gives abnormal results that don't indicate cancer but do frighten women, and thus afford gynecologists the opportunity to suggest unnecessary hysterectomies.

The technique of doing a Pap smear is simple and easily learned. It consists of lightly "scraping" the area around the opening of the cervix with a wooden or plastic spatula and wiping the spatula onto a glass slide. This is usually also done within the canal of the cervix and in the upper vagina.

When the slides are stained a pathologist can look at them under a microscope and examine the cells that were scraped from the surface. The pathologist's report reflects the degree of abnormality of these cells. In years past, the report would be in the form of a classification, class one through five. Now, however, that system is almost never used. The report will say either "normal" or "atypical," and include a comment about the degree and type of atypicality. Since the Pap smear is only a screening test and is not sufficient to make a tissue diagnosis, more must be done if the report is abnormal.

It's important to know that abnormal Pap smears do not necessarily indicate the presence of cancer. Many causes of abnormal smears are relatively innocuous. If you are told that your Pap was abnormal, be easily reassured by your doctor while further evaluation is planned. If the Pap smear showed cells that definitely were malignant, your doctor will be able to tell you so, but otherwise one of two things should be done. A Pap smear that suggests inflammation, and thus the possibility of a cervical infection, may be followed up by simply treating the infection, then repeating the Pap smear. If the infection was the only problem, the Pap should then be normal.

Any other abnormality on the smear must be further evaluated by a small biopsy of the cervix. Because the Pap smear cannot tell you exactly where on the cervix the abnormal cells came from, it was once routine to do many biopsies from the cervix, hoping to hit the spot that was abnormal. What was needed was a technique for determining the most abnormal spot on the cervix, so that a very tiny biopsy could be taken from that spot. There is now such a technique.

Colposcopy

The proper way to evaluate an abnormal Pap smear is to look at the cervix with an instrument called a colposcope. The colposcope looks like a set of binoculars on a stand and has a light source that can be switched between two colors. The procedure is similar to having a Pap smear, but with the additional discomfort of a biopsy.

After applying a solution to the cervix that makes the blood vessels in the surface of the cervix more prominent, the gynecologist looks at the area around the opening with magnification. With training, gynecologists can learn to recognize abnormal patterns of vessels that overlie different kinds of abnormality. By selecting the most abnormal area for biopsy, a doctor can be sure that the tissue report represents the worst thing present and that nothing more severe is being missed. That is true, however, only if the gynecologist knows that the entire area of abnormality in the cervix was visible during the colposcopy.

The biopsy itself consists of "biting off" a very tiny (about one millimeter) piece of tissue, using a biopsy instrument. The pain involved varies from a quick sharp pinch to a fairly severe pinch followed by cramping.

The tissue is sent to a pathologist, and in forty-eight hours or so a report is available that may make the diagnosis of cancer of the cervix or something less severe. The most common nonmalignant finding is a disorder known as dysplasia.

Cervical Dysplasia

Dysplasia is a disorder of the tissue that covers the surface of the cervix (the cervix is the so-called mouth of the womb, or uterus, which protrudes down into the top of the vagina). It has long been known that in its most severe form dysplasia is a precursor to cancer of the cervix, and that a significant number of women who have severe dysplasia will develop cancer if the uterus is left alone. Because it causes no symptoms whatsoever, dysplasia is only detected by a Pap smear, or by colposcopy and biopsy.

When diagnosed, dysplasia is described as "mild," "moderate," or "severe." Newer nomenclature uses the designations CIN I, II, or III. CIN stands for cervical intraepithelial neoplasia. For simplicity, I'll stick with dysplasia, but you should know that CIN I, II, and III are interchangeable with mild, moderate, and severe dysplasia.

For many years, patients with severe dysplasia have been told that the cause of dysplasia is unknown, but that a patient who has developed that kind of abnormal tissue is prone to continue to develop it. They were also told that it would eventually become cancer, and that therefore the entire uterus should be removed. Unfortunately, once dysplasia began to be understood, and a curative, painless, office treatment developed for it, the majority of gynecologists continued to recommend hysterectomy.

It is now certain that dysplasia represents changes in the cervical tissue that are caused by a viral infection, probably more than one of the many viruses that are transmitted sexually. This being the case, eradicating the affected tissue *and* the virus is a permanent cure and, in fact, such a treatment is now available, using the carbon dioxide laser.

The use of the laser in gynecology is now well established, and one of the most exciting uses for this tool is in the treatment of dysplasia. With a laser device mounted on a colposcope one can look at the cervix and, with the aid of magnification, see the areas of the cervix that the virus occupies and that have become dysplastic. Then the laser beam can be directed on these areas and the tissue vaporized. Not only does this eliminate the affected tissue *and* the virus, but it does it painlessly—thus without the need for any kind of anesthesia. It also can be done in the office, and it leaves no scarring.

The only time laser vaporization is not sufficient is when the doctor cannot directly see all of the affected area. Laser treatment is so good, in terms of benefit and effectiveness versus risk, that it is hard to understand why it is not standard treatment, and available in every gynecologist's office. The reasons become more clear on closer scrutiny.

Laser technology is relatively new in gynecology, and all but the most recently educated gynecologists must attend courses in laser physics and in the clinical applications of the laser before they can use it. The machinery itself is quite expensive. And what does a gynecologist get in return for this large investment of time and money? The gynecologist gets fewer two- or three-thousand-dollar hysterectomies to schedule.

The motivation to adopt this new technology is not compelling. Just as many older gynecologists avoid the additional training necessary to do new procedures, many others have chosen to ignore the opportunity to adopt new treatment techniques that threaten to reduce their income. Their patients, obviously, have no way of knowing that another treatment is available that is cheaper, less painful, and less risky but equally effective. *Demand* that you be referred to a physician trained to use the colposcope and laser. There is no acceptable alternative at present, the results are excellent, and the technique will save you a major operation. As with any treatment, there will be a small percentage of recurrences. Follow-up is necessary, but even in the small number of cases where an area of dysplasia recurs after laser vaporization, there is no new risk to the patient, and the treatment can simply be repeated.

Twenty-two

TUMORS, CYSTS, AND MASSES

ONE OF THE PURPOSES OF A PELVIC EXAM IS TO DETECT THE PRESENCE OF abnormal masses or lumps on or around the uterus, tubes, and ovaries. A mass may be an abnormal growth of tissue, in which case it is called a tumor. But it may be a normal growth of tissue or a mass of scar tissue and completely harmless. Here is a brief guide to some of the more common tumors and harmless masses and cysts.

Tumors of the Uterus

Tumors can be either malignant (cancerous) or benign (non-cancerous). Whether malignant or benign, a tumor is an abnormal growth of tissue that will continue to grow if unchecked. Malignant tumors of the uterus do occur and must be treated by surgery, radiation, or chemotherapy, depending on the type and stage. These tumors are relatively uncommon, and most of the tumors that develop in the uterus are so benign that they require no treatment at all. By far the most common of all tumors of the uterus is the fibroid. Except for very rare conditions, they are the only tumors of the uterus found in women younger than fifty. I briefly discussed fibroids in Chapter Seven, but since they are statistically listed as the most common reason for hysterectomy, and because there is so seldom a real necessity to treat them by hysterectomy, a thorough discussion is worthwhile.

Fibroids are properly called myomas (or myomata), from the Greek meaning "muscle tumor." Benign tumors, they arise from the muscle tissue that comprises all of the uterus but the thin inside and outside linings. No one knows what causes these tumors, but they are found, harmlessly, in about 40 percent of women. Varying in size from microscopic to huge, they need no treatment unless they are causing infertility, interfering with a pregnancy, or are so large as to cause discomfort. If they are close to the inside lining of the uterus, they may cause heavy periods.

Because they are most often harmless, you have to ask why they are statistically the most commonly listed indication for hysterectomy. The reasons are simple. A woman who is told she has "tumors" of the uterus is easily persuaded to have a hysterectomy by a financially motivated gynecologist. Also, in the large percentage of cases where hysterectomies are done needlessly, fibroids are found incidentally by the pathologist in many of the uteruses removed. Since that is the only "abnormality" listed on the final pathology report, gynecologists can cover themselves by listing the indication for hysterectomy as "uterine myomata."

You should understand, and believe, one thing: the presence of fibroids in your uterus is no cause for alarm. Neither is it a legitimate reason for surgery in and of itself. If the fibroids are causing symptoms that must be treated and there has been no success with medical types of treatment, then either hysterectomy or removal of the fibroids is appropriate. In recent years, the removal of fibroids from the uterus has become an easier and less complicated operation. This is largely a result of the use of the laser in the operation. Removal of only the fibroids, and not the uterus, should be the approach for anyone who wants to retain her uterus.

There is also a new type of hormonal medication available that can be used to treat fibroids or to enhance the safety and success of surgery. These drugs are the gonadotropin-releasing hormone analogs (Gn-RH analogs), and they are used for the suppression of endometriosis as well as for the temporary treatment of fibroids. They cause dramatic decrease in the size of fibroids, and can be administered prior to surgery to make removal of the fibroids easier. The current drugs and treatment regimens involve only temporary shrinkage of the tumors, however; the tumors will grow back to their original size within a few months after the drug is stopped. Since the drugs also cause a temporary and reversible menopause, long-term treatment with them is not yet feasible. But watch for the development of substances that can be used for a long time, or that produce a permanent decrease in the size of fibroids.

The only symptoms that require treatment for fibroids include bleeding heavy enough to cause iron-deficiency anemia, infertility due to mechanical obstruction by the fibroids, or fibroids of such size as to cause intolerable discomfort or harmful compression of other organs. If your fibroids grew large because of stimulation by birth-control pills or pregnancy, stopping the pills or completing the pregnancy will usually cause satisfactory regression, and no other treatment will be necessary.

Never believe that hysterectomy is the first, or even an appropriate, choice unless your doctor, and an objective second doctor, can explain to your satisfaction why that is the case.

Tumors of the Ovary

Tumors of the ovary are the most common kinds of tumors of the reproductive organs in women, and there are many, many types, some malignant, some benign. It is important to understand the difference between a real tumor, benign or malignant, and a functional cyst of the ovary. It is also important to know how a doctor should approach the finding of an enlarged ovary in any woman.

In the course of producing an egg each month, the ovary goes through a cycle of events in which the egg is matured inside a small cyst called a follicle. When the follicle ruptures at the time of ovulation, the egg is released by the ovary and picked up by the fallopian tube. The follicle itself, now called a corpus luteum, remains through the rest of the menstrual cycle and produces the hormone progesterone. This hormone acts on the lining of the uterus, causing changes that prepare it for receiving a fertilized egg. If fertilization doesn't occur, the follicle shuts down its production of progesterone. It is the sudden drop of progesterone levels in the blood that leads to the breakdown of the lining of the uterus and menstrual bleeding.

The importance of this series of events is this: During every menstrual cycle a cyst forms in the ovary! This cyst may even fill with a larger than usual amount of fluid, or fill with blood, and become fairly large. These cysts are called "functional" cysts of the ovary because they arise out of the normal function of the ovary. *They are not tumors.* They will resolve by themselves and need no treatment. When a doctor feels an enlarged ovary, the vast majority of the time, he or she is feeling a harmless functional cyst.

The dilemma for both doctor and patient, then, is when to leave an enlarged ovary alone and when to take action, such as looking into the abdomen with the laparoscope or opening the abdomen in a major operation. Tumors (neoplasms, or "new growths") of the ovary will continue to grow, and even the ones that are not cancerous will have to be removed. Functional cysts will go away on their own. Just knowing that an enlargement is cystic (hollow and filled with fluid), as opposed to solid, is not enough information, because some tumors, benign and malignant, can be cystic.

A few simple rules are used to decide whether to watch or act right away:

1. If the ovary is less than four centimeters in diameter, the growth is unlikely to be a tumor. Likewise, the larger it is beyond four centimeters, the greater the likelihood that it is a tumor.

2. If a woman is on birth-control pills the ovary does not go through the production of an egg and does not make functional cysts. If this woman has an enlarged ovary of any size, it should be investigated.

3. If a cyst fails to disappear after an entire menstrual cycle has passed, it is more likely to be a tumor. To be certain that a normal cycle has occurred, some physicians will give a course of birth-control pills or progesterone tablets and then, if the cyst persists, take a look at it.

The important thing is that harmless things should be left alone. Before surgery is performed, it must first be determined whether an enlarged ovary represents something abnormal.

Other Masses

In addition to the many types of tumors and the functional cysts of the ovary that may be discovered by a pelvic exam, there are other masses that can sometimes be felt, and can lead to confusion in diagnosis.

Women who have had pelvic surgery or who have had infections involving the tubes and ovaries may have resulting adhesions that bind structures together and make them feel like a solid mass. This can be hard to differentiate from a tumor.

Endometriosis can produce cystic tumors of the ovary, but it can also produce thickened areas on any structure in the pelvis. Like infection, endometriosis can cause adhesions that bind structures together into masses.

Most of the time it is possible to distinguish adequately the identity of a tumor, mass, or cyst by pelvic exam alone. When this is not the case, further information may be obtained by X ray, ultrasound, or blood tests. When these tools do not provide an adequate diagnosis, it is necessary to look into the abdomen for the final determination.

Questions to Ask

If you are presented with the finding of a mass inside the pelvis and the doctor recommends an operation, there are some questions to ask:

1. How big is it?
2. What are the most likely things it could be?
3. If it is one of those likely things, what would be the outcome if nothing is done? If surgery is done?
4. What other treatments or diagnostic procedures could be done?

After you have the answers to these questions, see another gynecologist for a second opinion. Be sure to explain that you want only an evaluation and advice, and that you do not want this doctor to do the surgery if surgery seems indicated. You may get a more unbiased answer about whether the surgery is necessary if the doctor's pocketbook is unaffected either way.

If, after the second opinion, you feel you should accept the recommendation of surgery, go back to the first doctor and do two things:

1. Be sure that the doctor will do the *least* surgery necessary, and do not give any written permission to do more. Many times, the least thing to do is to first look in with the laparoscope, and to proceed with opening the abdomen

only if something is seen that requires it. If something harmless is seen, you can have a nearly invisible one-half-inch scar, and go home the same day.

2. Tell your doctor that you would like to have a copy of the operative summary and the pathology report after the surgery is done. Plan to take that to another gynecologist to get an opinion of whether the surgery was appropriate and indicated. I recommend that you do this before any type of surgery, letting the doctor know that you plan to have the records examined. Doctors are much less likely to do anything unindicated if they know another doctor is going to review their actions and performance.

Twenty-three

COMMON CANCERS—CERVIX, BREAST, AND UTERUS

THE DISTINCTION BETWEEN A BENIGN TUMOR AND ONE THAT IS malignant (cancerous) lies in how the growth behaves if left alone. Benign tumors simply grow larger, and most will grow slowly. Malignant tumors will not only grow larger, they will grow rapidly. In addition, they will grow into, or "invade" adjacent tissue, and they will spread to distant organs, through the bloodstream or lymph channels, and continue to grow and invade there as well.

Benign tumors of the cervix, breast, and uterus are much more common than malignant ones, but cancer in any of these organs is potentially fatal. In all three areas, early detection and skillful treatment are essential to a good outcome.

I do not intend a thorough discussion of all types and stages of these cancers. My intent is to suggest the proper approach to their diagnosis and to the choice of treatment.

Cervical Cancer

More serious than cervical dysplasia is actual carcinoma (cancer) of the cervix. There are two distinct stages of this disease. The mildest form is called carcinoma in situ. The surface membrane of the cervix, about the thickness of a sheet of paper, is composed of many layers of cells. If the full thickness of this membrane is made up of malignant cells, but they do not extend into the deeper tissue, the disease is carcinoma in situ (from the Latin, meaning it has stayed in its original location).

If the malignant changes have penetrated more deeply than the surface, the disease is called invasive carcinoma of the cervix. This is much more serious because, once beyond the surface membrane, the cancer can spread to other areas through lymph channels and blood vessels.

Carcinoma in situ is appropriately treated by hysterectomy in a woman who wants no more children. However, in a younger woman who wants to retain the possibility of bearing children, a lesser treatment can be done. A conization of the cervix is performed, either with a scalpel, a laser, or a heated wire loop, and a large, cone-shaped piece of the cervix is removed. Studies of recurrence rates after various treatment modalities indicate that conization is curative almost 100 percent of the time.

If invasive carcinoma is present, the treatment should be hysterectomy, at least, and if the cancer has spread more deeply, or to other places, radiation treatments and/or a radical hysterectomy must be done. A radical hysterectomy involves removal of the uterus, tubes, and ovaries, plus the removal of all lymph nodes in the pelvis and all the loose connective tissue within which the nodes are located. The success of treatment depends on how far the disease has spread at the time of first detection.

Thanks in part to Pap smears, colposcopy, and the naturally slow growth of most cervical cancer, invasive cancer of the cervix is rarely seen today.

So, if you are found to have an abnormal Pap smear, don't panic, but be sure it is evaluated and treated properly:

1. Be sure your doctor is trained and experienced in colposcopy. If not, insist on a referral to someone who is.
2. If you are found, after colposcopy and biopsy, to have

mild, moderate, or severe dysplasia, or if the diagnosis is carcinoma in situ, ask to be referred to someone who is trained and experienced in the use of the laser.

3. Ask the treating physician to do the least treatment that will be effective, and ask that it be done without hospitalization and anesthesia, if possible.

Gynecologists have traditionally insisted that women should come to see them annually for a Pap smear. They persisted in this recommendation in spite of the American Cancer Society's strong statement that it is not necessary. Because of the variance in recommendations, in 1985 the American College of Obstetrics and Gynecology convened a task force to review guidelines for cancer-screening procedures. The result was a change in the official ACOG recommendation concerning Pap smears. ACOG now suggests that after a woman has had three consecutive annual Pap smears that are normal the test can be performed less frequently "at the discretion of her physician." The American Cancer Society had previously specified every three to five years but, as part of the task force, the society agreed to this compromise recommendation.

Many gynecologists, however, still instruct their patients to return annually. The underlying debate is interesting. Since it has been shown that cervical dysplasia and cervical cancer are related to sexually transmitted viruses, women who have had several years of negative Pap smears are not going to develop the disease if they are in a monogamous sexual relationship—thus the Cancer Society recommendation that those women need less frequent screening. Many gynecologists will not trust their patients to make the determination themselves, so instead of explaining the issue and having the patient come in for more frequent Paps if she has multiple or new sex partners, they just tell her that the safest thing is to have an annual Pap.

It is my opinion that the more exposure women have to gynecologists, the more uteruses will be removed, and I suspect that this is one of the underlying factors for the doctors who insist that their patients return for an annual Pap smear.

If you accept—and I do—that dysplasia and cancer of the cervix are virtually always caused by sexually transmitted viruses, the original Cancer Society recommendation makes sense. In research studies, genetic material from human papilloma viruses has been recovered from 90 percent of cervical cancers. Other studies have linked other types of viruses to cancer and dysplasia. With those findings, it is not unreasonable to assume that all cervical neoplasia is caused by some type of virus. Because of this, and because the time relationship between exposure and Pap smear changes, the Cancer Society had recommended that if a woman has one sex partner and has a normal Pap smear for two years running, she can wait five years before another.

On the other hand, if you or your current partner is ever sexually involved with someone else, or if there is some other reason to see a doctor annually, the additional cost of a Pap smear is negligible. Only one other screening test or routine physical-exam procedure I can think of has as much value for a woman, and it is intended for the early detection of breast cancer.

Breast Cancer

It is clear that women conscientiously performing breast self-exams each month are more effective at finding small breast lumps than are physicians performing one each year. More effective still is the use of the X-ray technique, now common and well known as mammography.

I strongly agree with the recommendation that, beginning at age thirty-five to forty, all women should have an annual mammogram. If you have a family history of breast cancer, especially in a mother or sister, this process should begin at the age of thirty. Annual mammograms, along with a low-fat diet and monthly breast self-exams, will give the best chance of avoidance, or very early detection, of breast cancer. There is no doubt that early detection is the key to curing the disease. There is also no doubt that simply having your gynecologist perform a breast exam each year is close to worthless. And self-examination is *not* a substitute for mammography.

Unfortunately, the enthusiasm for mammography has led to its being done in many facilities in which either the equipment or the people interpreting the test are substandard. The American College of Radiology established technical standards for mammography in 1990, but these are not applied nationally. Many X-ray facilities seek accreditation by these standards voluntarily. To determine what facilities in your area are accredited, you can call either the state office of the American Cancer Society or the National Cancer Institute.

Once you have had your first mammogram, make your annual mammogram a religious practice. Be sure that the person who will be interpreting the test has your previous test for comparison. This test, along with the Pap smear, can literally save your life. Little else that is done in the way of routine health screening has this high a value.

Uterine Cancer

Cancer of the uterus has become the most common cancer encountered by gynecologists. Almost 95 percent of these cases are cancers of the lining of the uterus, or endometrial cancer. The other 5 percent arise as one of the many types of sarcoma of the body of the uterus. The small number that remain are a combination of the two types.

The average age of women who develop cancer of the uterus is fifty-nine, so the vast majority are postmenopausal. Factors that predispose women to the development of uterine cancer include obesity, a low number of or no children, diabetes, and hypertension. Women who are given estrogen without the modifying effect of progesterone are also at an increased risk.

By far the most common symptom of endometrial cancer is abnormal bleeding. This can occur as heavier than normal periods, bleeding between periods, or bleeding without cessation. Any bleeding after menopause must be considered a possible sign of endometrial cancer and must be evaluated.

The evaluation of abnormal bleeding is by D and C. In a woman who is not yet menopausal, abnormal bleeding is unlikely to be related to cancer, and another form of sampling the tissue from the uterine lining is adequate. This could be done by endometrial washing or by a biopsy. A Pap smear is of no use in evaluating abnormal bleeding.

If you are postmenopausal and have any bleeding whatsoever, see a gynecologist. It must be checked out. If you are premenopausal and experience a significant change in your periods, it should be evaluated, as I discuss in Chapter Twenty-eight.

The rare forms of uterine cancer, such as sarcoma of the uterus, also occur primarily after menopause, at an average age of fifty-eight. The most common physical finding is an enlarged irregular-shaped uterus. Abnormal bleeding is the most common symptom, and it occurs in about 85 percent of patients. Less common symptoms include abdominal pain, weight loss, vaginal discharge, and a mass that you can feel in your lower abdomen. Treatment of this kind of cancer is not generally successful. Even when the cancer is found in its early stages only 50 percent of patients will survive five years. The only treatment that has been shown to have significant effectiveness is removal of the uterus, tubes, and ovaries. Adding radiation therapy or chemotherapy on top of surgery does not improve survival.

All forms of uterine cancer together constitute 7 percent of cancers in women. Your chance of developing this disease is hard to calculate because the incidence varies widely by location as well as race. White women in Iowa have an incidence of 21 in 100,000; Native American women in New Mexico, only 3.4 in 100,000; black women in New Orleans have a rate of 10.5 in 100,000.

Most important, abnormal bleeding prior to menopause is probably not cancer, and you should not let your doctor suggest any more radical diagnostic measures or treatment than necessary to remedy the situation.

Twenty-four

CONTRACEPTION

THE DECISION OF WHAT CONTRACEPTIVE TO USE IS A DIFFICULT ONE. Nothing that is now available is perfect, and no one contraceptive is the best choice for everyone. The choice is an individual one, and it should be made with as much information as possible. The considerations include your frequency of intercourse, the character of your menstrual cycles, your desire for future pregnancy, your level of comfort with various contraceptive devices, and your willingness to accept risk of complications or failure of the method.

Tubal Ligation

If a woman has reached a time in her life when she is certain that she will never again want to become pregnant, the best course of action is to have a tubal ligation. The decision should be made only if nothing could possibly happen that would change her mind, such as divorce and remarriage, the death of her children, or change in financial condition.

Once the decision for permanent sterilization has been made, a married couple should decide whether the husband should have a vasectomy or the wife a tubal ligation. Don't do it unless you genuinely want it to be permanent, and try to decide which spouse is most comfortable with the idea of permanent sterilization.

The wife, for instance, may be quite sure that she would not want to become pregnant again, no matter what might change in her life, while the husband may feel that if he lost his wife through divorce or death he might want the possibility of fathering a child with someone new.

Although it should be considered permanent, there is actually good success now with reversing sterilization operations in women, using microsurgical techniques. Depending on the type of tubal ligation done, the reversal can be successful up to 85 percent of the time. Vasectomies, however, are not as successfully reversed. Even though it is technically easier to repair a vasectomy so that sperm can once again pass through the vas deferens, the success rate if more than a year has passed since the vasectomy is less than 20 percent. The reason for this is that after vasectomy, the billions of sperm a man produces are absorbed by the body. The body treats them like a foreign substance and produces antibodies against them. Thus, if the vas is reopened, the sperm passing through have been crippled by the antibodies, and are not capable of fertilizing an egg.

There are many techniques of tubal ligation. Although the term means "tying the tubes," in none of the operations are they really just tied closed. In all of the commonly used techniques, a section of the tube is removed and the cut ends tied off.

The procedure can be done through a large incision in the abdomen at the time of a cesarean section or through a very small incision just above the pubic hair, or the laparoscope can be used. In this last technique, a one-half-inch incision is made in the bottom of the belly button, and the laparoscope is passed through it. While looking through the laparoscope, the physician inserts a second instrument through an even smaller incision and cauterizes a small segment of the tube on each side. This cauterized area disappears, leaving a gap in the middle of the tube.

The advantages of laparoscopic tubal ligation are the almost-invisible scar and the fact that a woman can have the procedure done as an outpatient, under anesthesia, and be able to go home the same day.

Do not let anyone talk you into a vaginal tubal ligation. In this technique an incision is made in the top of the vagina, and the tubes are approached that way. It is still done by some older physicians, but is quite prone to complications and is too risky to be considered.

An advantage of vasectomy is that it too is done as an outpatient procedure, using local anesthesia. Another advantage is that it is done to a man, one who has managed to avoid pregnancy and childbirth himself, and you may feel it is his turn.

Birth-Control Pills

While it has become increasingly clear that IUDs are not a safe form of contraceptive, birth-control-pill technology has steadily improved, and the pill can now be considered quite safe.

Birth-control pills contain two hormones: some type of estrogen and some type of progesterone. Both of these hormones, in their natural forms, are produced by the ovaries during normal menstrual cycles. When the synthetic forms are given throughout the cycle, a feedback occurs to the pituitary gland, which then shuts off production of the hormone that normally stimulates the ovary to produce an egg. With no egg produced, there can, obviously, be no pregnancy.

In the early days, no one knew how low the doses of these hormones could be and still do the job. Consequently, very high doses were used, and most of the ill effects of the pills were due to this. The current generation of pills are quite low in dosage, but still effective. Not only do they not cause the serious side effects they once were thought to cause, there is evidence that they actually have some positive effects.

Women who take birth-control pills have a lower incidence of breast cancer and uterine cancer. There is a wide variety of formulations of the pills, and a good gynecologist can select the right pill for the right woman so as to alleviate problems such as acne, menstrual cramps, heavy periods, and even, in some cases, excess facial-hair growth.

When beginning birth-control pills for the first time, be sure your doctor listens to your family history and your menstrual history, and then chooses the best pill for you, rather than giving you the same pill he or she always prescribes. There is a large variety of pills, with different amounts and types of the two hormones. Pills also vary as to the amount of each hormone that you get in particular times of your cycle. These different formulations will affect you differently, so the initial choice should be based on the nature of your cycles and the attendant symptoms that you experience with them. Be sure that your doctor plans to talk to you after the first two months on the pills, to learn how they have affected you. Most of the time, any negative effects can be alleviated by the proper change of pill, although there are certainly women who can never become satisfactorily adjusted to them, and they must turn to something else.

Barrier Methods of Contraception

The types of contraception that effect a barrier between sperm and cervix all have the positive quality of being fairly natural, with essentially no side effects. They all share one negative, however: a failure rate in the range of 10 to 15 percent. They also must be used at the time of intercourse, or just slightly in advance. Unanticipated sex may catch you unprepared if you haven't got your diaphragm or your foam and condoms with you. If you find the use of the device itself so unpleasant that you tend to avoid using it, then it obviously won't be your best choice for the long run.

The critical thing about all of these contraceptives is that they be used properly and, in the case of diaphragms and cervical caps, that they fit properly. The fit is solely dependent on the skill of the person doing the original fitting. If you find that your contraceptive is uncomfortable or slips out of place easily, go back for another fitting or a change of method.

Norplant

A new type of contraceptive has recently been introduced, and with it a great deal of fanfare. Its trade name is Norplant. It consists of five small cylinders, containing progesterone, that are implanted under the skin of the arm and remain there for five years. The cylinders release the progesterone slowly, and in sufficient amounts to reliably suppress the production of eggs. The mechanism of action is much the same as that of birth-control pills. The most attractive things about this method are that you need to take action only once each five years, and that the effect is reversible soon after the cylinders are removed.

On the negative side, the cost of the materials and insertion is quite high. Moreover, a large percentage of women who use it will experience abnormal bleeding of some kind. In my opinion, this side effect has not been well enough discussed in the frenzy of excitement over what is seen by some as another contraceptive for the "masses" who are unable to responsibly use other methods. Since Norplant cannot be fine-tuned like birth-control pills, you are pretty much stuck with whatever side effects it causes, unless you choose to have it removed, and thus sacrifice your initial investment. My advice is to be sure you understand the possible side effects and their frequency. If you would be unwilling to put up with those complications should they occur, Norplant is the wrong choice for you.

In a study at the University of Southern California School of Medicine, published in 1991, 234 Norplant users were followed for five years to chart their bleeding patterns and the rate of failure to prevent pregnancy. In the first year of use 66.3 percent of the women had irregular cycles. That improved over time, but by the fifth year 37.5 percent still reported irregular cycles. Ten of the women in the study became pregnant while using Norplant.

When seeking contraceptive advice, it is important that you ask whether your physician is unbiased about types of contraception. Many doctors don't believe in one form of birth control or another because of their religion or their personal experience. Male gynecologists may not be sufficiently understanding of a woman's experience with each method to understand the merits of each for you.

Whatever the doctor's bias, there should be no influence on your choice. Contraception must be tailored to your body, your life-style, your sex life, your preferences. If you receive the slightest hint that the doctor's preferences, biases, or convenience is involved, see someone else.

Twenty-five

SEXUALLY
TRANSMITTED
DISEASES AND
VAGINAL
INFECTIONS

"SEXUALLY TRANSMITTED DISEASE" IS A CATCHALL TERM FOR ANY DISEASE that is transmitted by sexual activity. In women, many show up as infections in the vagina and never become more than that. Some first appear as serious infections involving the internal reproductive organs, primarily the tubes and ovaries. A few can begin as vaginitis, then progress to involve other structures.

It's important to know about the common ones as well as the types of infection that give similar symptoms but are not transmitted sexually.

Vaginitis

"Vaginitis" means inflammation of the vagina, and many things can cause it. Let me describe the more common ones:

1. Herpes Simplex—This is a virus, the same one that causes the so-called cold sore that appears commonly on the lips or nose. Herpes simplex type I is responsible for infections above the waist 75 percent of the time, and type II is responsible for infections below the waist 75 percent of the time. Type I is also sometimes the cause of genital herpes, and type II is sometimes found in oral infections.

This virus can only be transmitted by direct contact with an active herpes sore. The fluid that seeps from the lesions of herpes is loaded with the virus, so that genital contact during intercourse leads to infection of the tissues of the vulva and vagina, and oral contact can lead to infection of the lips, tongue, or nose.

After a latent period, during which no symptoms are noticed, an initial lesion breaks out, usually as a painful craterlike sore. The lesion may be small and isolated, or sores may virtually cover the labia. Regardless of the severity of the initial outbreak, it usually clears within a few weeks, and the virus particles move away from the skin surface, down nerve fibers, where they lie dormant for some time.

Following the first episode, the disease acts quite unpredictably. It may never break out again (rarely), it may break out just before a menstrual period each month, or it may break out only when a woman is subjected to stress. The type of stress may be emotional, overall physical, or local, such as trauma to the vulva. Herpes simplex type I often erupts on the face after excess exposure to sunlight.

Because healthy bodies produce antibodies to combat viruses when they invade our tissues, each outbreak tends to be less severe, less painful, and shorter in duration than the first one. Nevertheless, since there is no drug as yet that kills the herpes virus inside the human body, anyone infected with it can assume they will have it in their tissues forever, perhaps to erupt as herpetic lesions often, perhaps virtually never. Some important facts to know:

A. You can give the infection to another person only while there is a lesion present.

B. Condoms will prevent spread to another person, presuming they don't leak or break.

C. The fluid from the lesions is the vehicle that contains and spreads the virus, so frequently washing your hands with soap during an outbreak helps prevent the spread.

D. Most women (and men) who have herpes can tell when it is about to break out and produce a lesion; they develop tingling or burning at the site prior to the outbreak (the lesions tend to recur each time at the same spot).

E. There is an ointment (acyclovir, brand name Zovirax) that does not cure herpes but, especially when applied prior to the outbreak, significantly lessens the severity of the lesions, as well as their duration. It is helpful with the facial cold sore as well.

2. Gardnerella—This bacterium causes one of the most common kinds of vaginal infection. Also called Hemophilus vaginalis, it is now known to be the cause of what was for years referred to as nonspecific vaginitis. You get it only from having intercourse with a man who is carrying it, and it virtually never causes symptoms in men. The diagnosis is made either by culture or by looking at a smear of vaginal discharge in a drop of saline under the microscope. You cannot see the organism, but you can see cells from the vaginal walls, which contain fragments of the bacteria. These telltale cells are called "clue cells."

The vaginitis is usually mild, with a grayish discharge and mild irritation. Medication with metronidazole (brand name Flagyl) will cure gardnerella, but the sex partner must be treated as well.

3. Trichomonas—This one-celled organism (a protozoan) causes a sexually transmitted infection that produces severe inflammation of the vagina, with a profuse, usually malodorous discharge, and can even make the cervix or the walls of the vagina bleed. Trichomoniasis is also one of the infections most likely to produce falsely abnormal Pap smears. The diagnosis is easily made by placing some of the vaginal discharge in a drop of saline and looking under the microscope. The trichomonads are easily seen, as they are much larger than bacteria, and move about rapidly.

The treatment is with metronidazole (brand name Flagyl), the same drug used for gardnerella. The dosage schedule is different for men and women, but it is critical that any sex partners, past or present, be treated during the same time period. The patient cannot consume any alcohol while taking the drug, because the combination causes severe nausea.

4. Chlamydia—Only recently has this well-known bacterium been recognized as a common cause of sexually transmitted gyn infection. Long known as the cause of the eye infection trachoma, chlamydia is so difficult to culture that, until recently, no research had been done to determine its frequency as an infection of the reproductive organs. There are now reliable culture and other diagnostic techniques, but they are still not as simple and quick as for other bacteria. Another problem with detecting chlamydia is that it is quite often asymptomatic.

In women it can produce a mild vaginitis or cervicitis or can quietly spread up to the uterus, tubes, and ovaries. Often it spreads without producing any warning symptoms and is discovered only in the course of an evaluation for infertility, when the tubes are found to be scarred closed (more about this type of infection shortly).

We now know that chlamydia is a *very* common infection, and should be looked for in any vaginal or cervical infection. After diagnosis, any past or present sex partners must be treated as well. Chlamydia is treated with a number of antibiotics, most commonly tetracycline or erythromycin, and requires a fairly long course of treatment for success.

5. Human Papilloma Virus (HPV)—This prevalent family of viruses includes strains that cause ordinary skin warts and is one of the most common viral causes of cervical dysplasia and cancer. In research studies it has been found in 90 percent of tissue samples of those diseases. Transmitted through sexual intercourse, it may manifest itself not only as dysplasia and cancer of the cervix but also as a type of wart called condylomata acuminata (more commonly called venereal warts).

These warts vary in size from tiny to huge and may be found anywhere on the vulva, on the perineum, in the vagina, or on the cervix. Men may have such tiny ones on their genitalia as to be almost invisible, but it is certain that if a woman develops these warts, she has gotten them from a sex partner who already had them, and the partner must be treated also.

In the past, the only treatments were to apply a chemical called podophyllin to the infected area or to surgically remove the warts. Today, a new and effective method utilizes the laser. It leaves less scarring than scalpel surgery and can be used through the colposcope, allowing the laser surgeon to see even microscopic warts. If these are not all destroyed, a cure will not be effected.

Since the laser has become available, an unfortunate side issue has arisen in the treatment of this disease. Few dermatologists yet use the laser, and most of the people trained to use the type of laser appropriate for treating venereal warts are gynecologists. Since the only effective treatment includes treatment of the male sex partners as well, gynecologists have been in a quandary as to who should take responsibility for this side of the treatment. It is hoped that either dermatologists or, more appropriately, urologists will fill this gap. In any case it is critical for you, the patient, that *someone* evaluates and treats your sexual partner(s).

Because of the failure rates and the pain involved with all of the currently available treatments for this disease, a new approach is badly needed. Ideally, modern science will develop a treatment that will attack the virus itself wherever it exists, without the need to surgically approach each wart. Because of the stimulus to research on viruses brought about by AIDS, such a treatment may be available in the near future. Look for either a drug that attacks the virus directly or something that provokes the patient's immune system to destroy the virus itself.

6. Monilia—Probably the most common form of vaginitis is not transmitted sexually at all. Yeast, or monilia, infections arise because this fungus is normally present in many places, including the vagina. When conditions become right for it to grow, it flourishes and produces severe itching, a thick white discharge, and a "yeasty" vaginal odor. The most common conditions in which an infection will occur involve heat and humidity (for example, traveling to hot and humid climates or wearing clothes that trap heat, such as nylon panties, panty hose, swimsuits, and workout clothes).

Fortunately, yeast infections are easily treated with a vaginal cream or suppository containing one of several antifungal agents. In the small percentage of cases that don't respond quickly or that recur, an oral drug is used. This is done with the assumption that reinfection is occurring from the presence of yeast in the rectum. Rarely, persistent yeast infections may be caused by an undiagnosed case of diabetes. In the vast majority of cases, however, treatment is simple. Self-diagnosis is easily done by any woman who has had a yeast infection, and over-the-counter medication is now available without a prescription in the form of Monistat or Gyne-Lotrimin.

This is not a complete inventory of the organisms that cause vaginitis, but it includes the common and important ones and all the commonly occurring sexually transmitted ones. Syphilis, though on the rise again, has already received plenty of attention in the past. Gonorrhea certainly can present only with symptoms of vaginitis, but I have included it in the next section because its appearance as an infection of the tubes and ovaries is its most devastating behavior.

Pelvic Inflammatory Disease

When infection involves the internal organs of the reproductive system, primarily the fallopian tubes and the ovaries, it is called pelvic inflammatory disease. When it first occurs, and the infectious agent is present and actively inflaming these structures, it is called acute pelvic inflammatory disease (usually shortened to acute PID). The symptoms of this disorder vary in intensity with the type of organism causing the infection but generally include lower abdominal pain and tenderness, fever, and frequently nausea, diarrhea, and severe pain with intercourse.

If you were to look inside the pelvis during this acute phase of the infection you would see pus coming from the ends of the tubes, and the surfaces of the uterus, tubes, and peritoneum (the membrane that lines the abdominal cavity) would appear quite red.

Even if PID is diagnosed and effectively treated, or if the cause is eliminated by the body's immune system, the damage left behind can produce a syndrome called chronic PID. No longer is the infectious agent present, and no longer is there active production of pus and redness, but the tubes and ovaries are involved with adhesions and, in fact, everything in the pelvis may be stuck together. The fallopian tubes are almost always sealed closed on their ends, and may be filled with fluid and stretched into functionless small water balloons.

Chronic PID may be asymptomatic, or it may cause irregular menstrual periods, painful intercourse, and intermittent pelvic pain.

Many years ago, acute or chronic PID was synonymous with gonorrhea, because that was the only kind of infection that we knew to cause it. Now we know that the infection may be a result of gonorrhea, chlamydia, tuberculosis, some fungi (not monilia), and, especially if an IUD has been in place, bacteria like streptococcus, bacteriodes, or staphylococcus. Whatever the cause, the diagnosis must be made and appropriate and aggressive treatment begun quickly to prevent the development of chronic PID and possible infertility or crippling pelvic pain.

Treatment consists of antibiotic therapy, the choice of antibiotic depending on the organism involved. If the symptoms are mild, oral antibiotics are sufficient. When the infection is acute and severe, especially if there are signs of peritonitis (inflammation of the lining of the abdomen), hospitalization and intravenous therapy with high doses of antibiotics are indicated.

AIDS

I can add nothing to the massive amount of information available concerning AIDS, but one aspect of this disease seems appropriate to mention here. As I write, the AMA and the American College of Surgeons have just announced that they will formally oppose mandatory testing of physicians for the HIV virus.

It seems to me that a woman has the right to know if a physician, who will be doing procedures on her that might transmit a fatal disease, is carrying that disease. Just as you have the right to know if your spouse or sex partner carries the HIV virus (and to decide if you wish to take the risk of sex with them, using condoms), you have the right to know if your doctor has it, and if you are willing to trust his or her procedures for avoiding its spread to you. (If you don't believe that doctors engage in high-risk sex and inject drugs just as other people do, you have missed the point of this book so far.)

To suggest that it is not your right to know is another example of the incredible arrogance of the medical profession, and of their disdain for you. I sincerely hope that either malpractice-insurance carriers or the government will have addressed the issues of mandatory testing and disclosure by the time this book is published, and will have found a way to require that physicians and other health-care professionals capable of infecting a patient with AIDS be tested and the results made public.

AIDS is yet another plague in the long series that has threatened human beings since recorded civilization began. It has not yet caused the decimation of large populations that resulted from smallpox, syphilis, and cholera, but the virus is present in approximately one million Americans today. It is spread through sexual contact, both homosexual and heterosexual, through contaminated needles, and from mother to child during pregnancy. The fastest growing category, proportionately, is that of heterosexual spread. No one can be considered safe from this disease if they engage in sexual intercourse with anyone who has ever done it before.

Until recently, the popular wisdom held that AIDS was a disease of homosexual men and drug addicts, and that the majority of Americans were exempt from risk. Those infected were too easily dismissed by the medical establishment, and there is arguably a case that this resulted in less aggressive efforts to combat the disease. As with women's health care, bias and stereotyping by the medical profession has had a detrimental effect on research, diagnosis, and access to care for those on the receiving end.

In the area of sexually transmitted diseases, women are most directly subjected to the gender biases of their doctors. When sexuality is involved, gynecologists may bring their sexist thinking into the treatment setting and let their own problems affect their patients. Sexually transmitted diseases are common and should be approached with the same perspective as any other infectious disease.

By asking the right questions you can be sure that you are being diagnosed and treated appropriately. By being sensitive to it, you can recognize the first hint of sexism in the gynecologist's office, and confront it. There is always another choice of provider, and you don't have to accept abuse in order to receive treatment.

Questions to Ask

If you see a doctor for symptoms of vaginal discharge, itching, or discomfort, for lower abdominal pain and fever, or for any other situation that leads him or her to tell you that you have a vaginal infection, cervicitis, or PID, there are things you need to ask:

1. What do I have, specifically, by name?
2. How did I get it?
3. If I got it from my husband or sex partner, how did *he* get it?
4. *When* did I get it, and how long could he have been carrying it?
5. How have you made the diagnosis, and how certain is it?
6. Can you be certain that I don't have more than one kind of infection?
7. How will you confirm that it is cured?
8. What are the possible aftereffects, and will it be possible to determine if I've suffered any?
9. How will my husband or partner be treated, and by whom?
10. Is this the kind of sexually transmitted disease that should make me worry that my husband or partner might also carry some other kind of infection?
11. When, and in what circumstances, will it be safe for me to have sex again?

Twenty-six

ENDOMETRIOSIS AND MENSTRUAL CRAMPS

THE LINING OF THE UTERUS IS CALLED THE ENDOMETRIUM (FROM THE Latin for inside the uterus). It is a specialized, glandular tissue that responds to the hormones from the ovaries by thickening and changing throughout the menstrual cycle, preparing to receive a fertilized egg.

If fertilization and implantation of an egg does not occur, the endometrium breaks down and sloughs off with menstrual bleeding. Endometriosis (-osis at the end of a word means condition) is a disease in which that same type of tissue is found *outside* the uterus, as implants in abnormal locations. These growths may be found on the tubes and ovaries, on the surface of the uterus, on the bowel, on the bladder, or behind the uterus, in the cul-de-sac just in front of the rectum.

Wherever it occurs, this tissue acts just like endometrium, responding to the hormones from the ovaries, and actually bleeds a little with the menstrual period. Most important, it also produces a chemical substance called prostaglandin that has very potent effects on surrounding tissues, such as the uterus or bowel.

In part, how the tissue acts depends on where it is and how much of it there is. Some women have very severe symptoms with very little endometriosis, and other women have severe endometriosis with mild or no symptoms. Typical symptoms include premenstrual pain, menstrual pain, lower abdominal tenderness, and pain with intercourse, especially near the beginning of the menstrual period. Most women with endometriosis experience excessive premenstrual abdominal bloating, and some women also have bowel symptoms, such as painful bowel movements, gas, cramping, or diarrhea. All symptoms commonly become worse just before a menstrual period. Endometriosis is one of the most frequent causes of infertility, and can cause it even if the disease is very minimal.

Endometriosis is such a variable disease that the array of symptoms can include many other things as well. No one understood its behavior at all until it was discovered that prostaglandins were produced by implants of endometriosis. The amounts produced exceed that produced by the normal endometrial lining of the uterus (the prostaglandins produced by normal endometrium cause so-called normal menstrual cramps). One of the current major theories suggests that the extra prostaglandins act on the adjacent tissues and cause symptoms like bowel cramping, uterine cramping, and nausea.

It's interesting to note that one of the current means of intentionally inducing abortion involves giving women suppositories of prostaglandin, causing violent uterine cramps and miscarriage. It is well documented that women with untreated endometriosis who manage to get pregnant have a significantly greater frequency of miscarriages . . . prostaglandins?

Although the actual cause of endometriosis is not agreed upon, many predisposing factors are well known. These include the presence of fibroids in the uterus, a small cervical canal (which causes greater pressures inside the uterus during cramping), and previous abortion or D and C. It is clear that in many women fragments of endometrium pass backward out through the end of the tubes during menstruation and that these fragments are able to grow where they land and persist as implants of endometriosis.

However, endometriosis is also found in places like the belly button, where this mechanism would clearly be impossible. The probable explanation is that embryonic tissue, once capable of becoming any kind of tissue, was stimulated by unknown factors to become endometrial tissue. Research has recently focused on an apparent involvement of the immune system in the development of endometriosis. Whatever the cause, it is clear that endometriosis depends on the production of estrogen for its sustenance, because it becomes inactive and asymptomatic at menopause.

Small implants of endometriosis look like tiny charred spots; they are black with puckering of the surrounding tissue. When endometriosis involves the ovaries, it forms cysts that gradually fill with old blood and can become quite large. The old blood turns black and thick, which is why these cysts are called chocolate cysts, as well as endometriotic cysts or endometriomata.

The treatment of endometriosis depends upon the symptoms in each case, what the goals of treatment are, and the age of the patient. It can be treated by drugs or by surgery, both of which offer some degree of success.

The most effective surgical treatment, in my opinion, is the use of the laser to "vaporize" the implants of endometriosis. This method was first used by aiming a hand-directed laser on the areas of endometriosis after the abdomen had been opened.

Lasers have now been developed that can be fired through a laparoscope, so that implants of endometriosis can be vaporized through a one-half-inch incision in the bottom of the navel. This technique is already available in some places using the carbon dioxide laser, and is very promising. A different kind of laser, the argon laser, is in the initial stages of clinical use. As I said in an earlier chapter, however, it will be a long time before a majority of gynecologists have obtained the necessary training to use lasers safely and well.

221

Other treatments have been tried unsuccessfully, such as suppression of menstrual periods with progesterone, or birth-control pills. Besides laser surgery, the only other treatment with significant success utilized one of two types of drugs. The first, a synthetic derivative of the male hormone testosterone, goes by the brand name Danazol. It suppresses the endometriosis but is not a cure, and it has many side effects. Most of these side effects it shares with the second group of drugs, which include the previously mentioned Gn-RH analogs. These latter drugs, one brand name of which is Nafarelin, act, as does Danazol, to bring about a reversible menopause. The idea is that temporary suppression of the areas of endometriosis might result in the possibility of pregnancy, or might suppress symptoms sufficiently to obviate any need for other treatment.

It is important for you to understand that if you use one of these medical treatments which simulate the effect of menopause, you will also experience the other symptoms of menopause while you take the drug. Also, after completing the drug treatment you will not be "cured" of endometriosis; you will have only suppressed its symptoms for an unpredictable length of time. It will still be present, though causing less trouble. The rationale for choosing these drugs is the hope that you might become pregnant during the temporary suppression period; or, if surgery is planned, the drugs may be used to try to make the endometriosis more amenable to surgery.

The reason for choosing surgery instead of drugs is that in many cases you can eliminate all the endometriosis that is present. Surgery will not prevent you from developing endometriosis again in the future, however, unless your uterus has been removed. But many women treated with conservative (nonhysterectomy) surgery will not develop significant endometriosis again in their lifetime, and many infertility patients will go on to have more than one pregnancy without further treatment. An argument against using drugs prior to surgery is that they can make the areas of endometriosis more difficult to see and eliminate.

The presence of endometriosis can often be determined by a pelvic exam alone. Most of the time, however, a laparoscopy must be done, so that the implants can be seen. It is also necessary to look inside to determine where the implants are, how much scarring has occurred, and thus what treatment approach would be best.

The existence of endometriosis was known about long before there was much accurate information about who had it, how they got it, how it acted, or how it should be treated. Many erroneous theories and myths were published, as well as theories about the women who were most often its victims. This misinformation caused many misdiagnoses. Every woman is a potential endometriosis victim, and while the disease is still difficult to treat successfully, there are an increasing number of treatment alternatives, and thus an increasing number of factors to consider before consenting to any type of treatment.

Questions to Ask Yourself

If faced with the diagnosis of endometriosis, you must give your doctor some information before you ask the crucial questions.

1. Do you plan to ever try to get pregnant, or do you want to maintain that option? Be sure your doctor knows how important that is!
2. Do you want to take your best chance at getting pregnant *now,* or do you hope to have children some years in the future?
3. How bad are your symptoms now? Are they tolerable or must you have immediate relief?
4. If you would rather live with your symptoms than risk

treatment, be sure your doctor understands that; sometimes endometriosis simply does not progress and at menopause becomes asymptomatic or totally disappears.

Questions to Ask Your Doctor

Once you are sure your doctor understands your needs and desires, ask these things:

1. What treatment do you recommend?
2. What other treatment possibilities are there, and why do you recommend this one over the others?
3. If the treatment involves surgery, will you use the laser?
4. Are you trained in infertility surgery, microsurgery, and laser surgery?
5. What are the chances of success with each form of treatment? What are the side effects, and the possible complications, of each?

I cannot stress strongly enough that any surgery for endometriosis be done by someone who is trained in the latest surgical techniques. These methods will help avoid postoperative adhesions, cause the least damage to reproductive organs, and maximize the chances that these organs will be functional after surgery. This training should include experience in infertility surgery, microsurgery, and the use of the laser in surgery. More about these techniques in Chapter Twenty-nine.

Dysmenorrhea

Painful periods are certainly one of the most common afflictions of women, and the treatment has changed so dramatically that it is important for you to know that help is available.

Menstrual cramps are among the many things long misunderstood, and mistreated, by gynecologists, undoubtedly because gynecologists have been predominantly males who never experience them. Historically, cramps have been attributed to personality disorders, stress, malpositions of the uterus, imagination, and many other equally unfounded causes.

Two things are now well known: that women who experience severe cramping with their menses have measurably stronger contractions of the uterus during periods than women who don't (in other words, they have real cramps, in their uteruses, not their heads); and that the cramping of the uterus is caused by prostaglandins, substances produced by the lining of the uterus, with the peak production occurring just prior to menstrual bleeding.

The body actually produces many kinds of prostaglandins, with effects on different tissues. The breakthrough in treatment for menstrual cramps came about through the study of other disorders whose symptoms were also caused by prostaglandins. These substances also produce the inflammation experienced in arthritis, and the drugs used successfully to alleviate the pain of arthritis turned out to inhibit the action of prostaglandins.

When this knowledge was applied to dysmenorrhea, it was found that antiarthritis drugs would, in fact, work quite well for menstrual cramps. It was not long before the most effective drugs for opposing the specific prostaglandins involved in dysmenorrhea were identified. There are now a number of them on the market. (They might have been here sooner if male gynecologists had had menstrual cramps higher on their list of priorities.) The drugs include the brands Anaprox, Dolobid, Motrin, Nalfon, Naprosyn, Nuprin, Ponstel, and others. Aspirin, in fact, has some antiprostaglandin activity.

These drugs are remarkably effective, and they have only one common side effect. Many women experience such severe stomach pain from taking prostaglandin-inhibitors that they are unable to use them. Unfortunately, these drugs are so closely related that if you have trouble with one, you probably will have trouble with all.

If these drugs don't bother you but don't help either, it is worth considering whether you have some cause for your menstrual cramps other than the usual, or functional, dysmenorrhea. The possibilities include endometriosis, fibroid tumors of the uterus, or congenital abnormalities of the uterus or cervix. Try the drugs first, but if they don't work, ask your doctor to pursue it further.

Another thing to remember is that birth-control pills virtually always eliminate menstrual cramps, so if you have cramps and need contraception, there's a good case for the pill. If you are taking pills but still have cramps, there is a good chance you have endometriosis, or something else.

Twenty-seven

INFERTILITY

IN THE UNITED STATES, 3.5 MILLION (17 PERCENT) OF MARRIED COUPLES have some infertility problem, and that number, for many reasons, is increasing. In about 40 percent of the cases, problems can be attributed to the male partner, in 40 percent to the female partner, and in 20 percent to the couple (physical, emotional, or sexual incompatibility of some kind between the specific individuals). In the female partner there are a number of possible causes. Abnormal ovulation accounts for about 15 percent. Tubal factors, including adhesions from previous infection or surgery, and endometriosis account for 25 to 30 percent. Immunologic incompatibility is found in 5 percent, and nutritional or metabolic factors in another 5 percent. Because multiple factors may be involved, all possible causes must be addressed.

Advances in infertility diagnosis and treatment have moved faster than perhaps any other area in the specialty of ob-gyn. For this reason, fewer and fewer physicians are genuinely competent to handle all areas of infertility treatment equally well. If you need help with an infertility problem, see a physician with advanced training, not just a board-certified ob-gyn specialist.

There is only one subspecialty board certification related to infertility, and that is in reproductive endocrinology. Few people have obtained this certification, and most of them are in academic settings, such as teaching hospitals and large medical centers. For the initial evaluation of infertility, you should look for a board-certified ob-gyn specialist who advertises as an infertility specialist; at your first meeting, ask what type of training the physician has had in this field.

There are two types of training to look for. The most reliable, but not common in private practice, is a postgraduate *fellowship* in infertility. This is an extra year or more of specialty training, after the ob-gyn residency, dedicated solely to the study of infertility.

Most commonly, you will find that a gynecologist interested in infertility will have obtained extra training by attending a series of postgraduate courses. An infertility specialist should have attended a number of these, and will probably be a member of the American Fertility Society. Because the treatment of infertility is so technologically advanced, specific types of treatment require specific training, even beyond postgraduate training in infertility. Let me describe some of the advanced areas of infertility treatment and tell you what training to look for if you become involved in any of these treatments.

The development of microsurgery has contributed greatly to success in the treatment of infertility. It would seem that "microsurgery" should refer to operations on very small structures, but the word is actually used to mean surgery that is done with the aid of magnification. Pioneered primarily by the field of ophthalmology, microsurgery is now widely used in neurosurgery and plastic surgery, as well as in gynecology.

Microsurgery has expanded the visual horizons of gynecologic surgeons, so that not only can they handle small structures more aptly but they can better understand the effects of their surgical actions on the reproductive structures of women. The result has been a realization that every *touch* upon a tissue, not just every cut, suture, or tear, has dramatic aftereffects. We now know that most of the surgical techniques of the past caused the formation of adhesions, the impairment of tubal or ovarian function because of altered anatomy, and, often, subsequent infertility. Even when the surgery was performed to treat infertility, it often did more harm than good.

Good gyn surgeons have adopted the techniques learned from microsurgical research in every aspect of their surgical practice, improving results in hysterectomy and surgery on other reproductive organs. Less conscientious gynecologists have continued their old techniques, and they continue to cause harm, greater postoperative pain, and more complications from their operations.

In addition to the overall contribution to the improvement of gynecologic surgery techniques, in two specific areas microsurgery has brought about improved results: the reversal of voluntary sterilization (tubal ligation) and the repair of tubes and ovaries damaged by infection or previous surgery (tuboplasty).

Tubal Reanastomosis

With proper training and experience, a good microsurgeon can now successfully repair tubes previously divided, tied, or partially destroyed and bring about restored fertility in over 70 percent of cases. Since so many women have tubal ligations done, only to change their minds about childbearing years later, this has been a precious contribution to the opportunity to give women their own choices, and control over their own reproductive lives.

The success rate varies depending on the technique of tubal ligation that was done, and any young woman having a tubal ligation should be certain that her gynecologist agrees to (and knows how to) do the procedure in such a way as to maximize the opportunity for reversal if she should ever so desire.

Tuboplasty

Prior to microsurgical techniques, a woman who had tubes that were scarred closed or rendered unable to function because of adhesions caused by previous infection had almost no chance of successfully having an operation restore her ability to conceive. Depending on the degree and type of damage, the results are still not ideal, but success rates have increased fourfold with microsurgery.

The key thing to know is that microsurgery done by someone with improper training, experience, and ability is worthless. Proper training in microsurgery involves technical training in a microsurgery laboratory, clinical training with good microsurgeons to learn proper application of the techniques, and experience.

If you are faced with the need for surgical reversal of sterilization or surgical treatment of infertility, do not let it be done by anyone without extensive training and experience. Your doctor should not be offended by your asking for his or her credentials. In addition, if someone better is available to you, go to that person. Just as is true in so many kinds of surgery, success in microsurgery is directly proportionate to experience and ability.

You should look for formal microsurgery laboratory training and postgraduate courses in the clinical application of microsurgery; then ask the physician how many microsurgical procedures he or she performs routinely. Anyone who does less than one a week probably does not keep their skills sharp, and anyone who has been doing it less than a year is probably not going to be very good at it yet. If no one in your town has the right credentials, it is worth a trip to a teaching hospital or large medical center for this type of surgery. Your doctor should be able to help you arrange this.

I have previously described the use of the laser in treating disease of the cervix, venereal warts, and endometriosis. In addition to endometriosis treatment, there is one other area of infertility treatment where the laser offers much promise.

As I have already discussed, adhesions between structures in the pelvis can be caused by infection or surgery on reproductive organs. These adhesions result in infertility either because the tubes are completely closed and an egg cannot pass into them from the ovary, or because the structures are so fixed in abnormal positions that the normal pickup of an egg by the tube cannot occur.

In the past, surgery to free these adhesions or reopen the tubes was fairly unsuccessful because the surgery itself caused further adhesion formation. In conjunction with the use of microsurgery, many infertility surgeons are using the laser in place of scissors or scalpel. This gives them an extremely precise tool that can be directed through the microscope, damages tissue less, and leads to less adhesion formation.

Studies concerning the effectiveness of the laser in the prevention of adhesions are ongoing, and the results are not yet conclusive. There is no question, however, that a physician who uses all of the techniques that have been developed by microsurgeons and laser surgeons has better results than one who employs only routine surgical skills.

In Vitro Fertilization and Embryo Transfer

The most exotic, expensive, and difficult of all infertility treatments is the "test-tube baby" process. In this procedure an infertile woman is given drugs to make her produce one or more eggs. The eggs are retrieved from the ovary through the laparoscope and then fertilized with the husband's sperm in a culture medium. When the fertilized egg has divided many times, is now technically an embryo, and has achieved the stage of maturation at which it normally reaches the uterine cavity and implants, it is taken from the culture dish and placed into the cavity of the uterus through the cervix.

In order to improve the success rate of the procedure, several years ago doctors decided to implant all the eggs that were successfully fertilized and had divided. This now-standard practice often causes multiple births—twins, triplets, quadruplets, or even more. This, along with the staggering cost and low success rate, is the major risk of the procedure.

The process is recommended for women whose fallopian tubes are irreparably damaged, or when microsurgical repair has failed. As success rates improve, in vitro fertilization will be used to treat other causes of infertility where current techniques have lower success rates.

If you are a candidate for in vitro fertilization, there is no choice but to go to a major medical center capable of performing all the surgical and technological tricks necessary to bring about this extraordinary feat. Your choice of facility should be made on the basis of its cost and success rate. Success rates vary from less than 5 percent to near 20 percent. Remember, however, that it may cost thousands of dollars to try it in *one* menstrual cycle; that if it fails, as it does about 90 percent of the time, you must start over again, both with the procedures and the costs; and that the odds of success are the same with each menstrual cycle.

A friend of mine operates a clinic where this procedure is done. He tells me that some patients take second mortgages on their homes to fund this procedure, even though he's told them that this is like betting the family farm on a horse with a 5 percent chance of winning.

New variations on this technique are now being applied for particular types of rare infertility situations. It is possible to take an egg from the ovary, place it into a fallopian tube that is blocked on its end, and have it naturally fertilized by intercourse or artificial insemination. The egg is placed into the tube through the uterine cavity, or directly through the wall of the tube with a needle.

In another procedure an embryo is taken from one woman's

uterus and implanted into the uterus of an infertile patient, who then carries it to term.

Needless to say, these things are quite new, expensive, and rare, and some of them are being tried in only a few places in the world. There is little danger of having this procedure recommended to you inappropriately, but let me repeat that new institutions are beginning to do these things all the time. It takes a great deal of experience for a team to become proficient, so check their track record before you commit. Also be sure that your doctor is not leapfrogging conventional infertility treatment that might work for you in order to perform a more exotic and expensive procedure.

As a general rule, the high-tech, expensive types of infertility treatments are best done in major medical centers with long experience. If a local physician claims to be able to duplicate the success rate of these centers, be skeptical. A lot of gynecologists out there do this type of treatment inappropriately and inadequately because the fees are quite large.

Twenty-eight

ABNORMAL BLEEDING AND D AND C

IN YEARS PAST, ALMOST EVERY WOMAN WHO HAD IRREGULAR, HEAVY, OR painful menstrual bleeding was subjected to a D and C. With increasing knowledge about the hormonal control of menses and the use of hormonal substances to treat abnormal bleeding, the usefulness of a D and C has become negligible, but they are still done with distressing frequency.

There are two possible reasons to do a D and C: to remove tissue from the uterine lining in order to make a diagnosis (called a diagnostic D and C) or to scrape out abnormal tissue in order to stop bleeding (a therapeutic D and C).

A diagnostic D and C can often be done in the office, for $200 to $400 plus the fee for the pathologist to look at the tissue removed. Since the procedure takes little time for the doctor, it presents the most dangerous of medical situations: a high ratio of money earned to time spent by the physician.

Here are the times when a therapeutic D and C should be done:

1. After a spontaneous abortion (miscarriage), to remove the fragments of placental tissue that are virtually always left behind and will continue to cause problems if not removed.

234

2. After a delivery when continued hemorrhage suggests retained placental fragments.
3. When hemorrhaging from the uterus is so rapid that the
   patient's life would be endangered in the time it might take
   to wait for hormonal treatment to work.
4. When an IUD must be removed from the uterus but the
   string has broken, so that the IUD cannot be grasped with
   an instrument and must be scraped out.
5. When medical (hormonal) treatment has failed to correct
   abnormal bleeding.

Here are the times when a diagnostic D and C should be done:

1. In any woman who has vaginal bleeding after menopause.
2. In a woman of any age who has bleeding that persists in
   spite of appropriate treatment with hormones. In those
   women cancer of the uterine lining, or precancer, must be
   ruled out.

Hormonal Treatment of Abnormal Bleeding

The hormonal mechanisms that control the reproductive cycle of
preparation of the uterine lining, production of an egg, and bleeding
if no pregnancy occurs are well known. The chain of hormonal
interactions begins with hormones produced in the brain that act on
the pituitary gland. The pituitary gland produces hormones that act
on the ovaries; the ovaries respond by producing an egg each cycle,
and by producing the hormones that target the lining of the uterus
(endometrium), and thus control the cycle of monthly bleeding.

Although all of the hormones involved are known, not all
have been either synthetically produced or isolated from tissues.
Our knowledge of the whole process is still at such an early stage
that most of our treatment is not sophisticated enough to attack the

origin of the problem. We must treat the problem further down the line, essentially treating the symptoms, not the disease. Let me explain how that is done.

There are two hormones, estrogen and progesterone, that we understand well and can produce easily, and both are produced by the ovary.

Estrogen, in an average twenty-eight-day menstrual cycle, is produced throughout the entire cycle. Its action is to cause the lining of the uterus to thicken, and to grow new blood vessels.

Progesterone is produced only in the second half of the cycle, the half between the release of an egg from the ovary (ovulation) and the next menstrual period. It is produced by the follicle in which the egg developed, and its action is to mature the uterine lining so that when an egg, having been fertilized by the sperm in the fallopian tube, reaches the uterine cavity, the lining is ready to receive it and support its development of a placenta. If no fertilized egg implants, the ovary shuts down production of progesterone. The sudden drop in the amount of progesterone in the bloodstream is what causes the lining of the uterus to break down, bleed, and slough off during the menstrual bleeding. Then the whole process begins again.

Whenever this elaborate process malfunctions and abnormal bleeding occurs, it is called "dysfunctional uterine bleeding." When the hormonal processes are working normally but there is some structural abnormality causing the bleeding, the abnormal bleeding is said to be "organic" in its cause. The treatment of each condition is different.

Dysfunctional Uterine Bleeding
This type of bleeding may show up as heavier than normal menses, longer than normal menses, bleeding between periods, or continuous bleeding throughout the cycle. By itself, it is harmless and rep-

resents no threat; treatment is aimed at correcting either the loss of blood or the inconvenience, or both. Most dysfunctional bleeding actually has its origin in abnormal production of hormones by the brain, but we don't know how to treat that directly. The usual result, however, is for the ovary to fail to produce an egg and thus fail to produce progesterone. The lining of the uterus is not regularly sloughed off and replaced, and starts to bleed abnormally.

Scraping out the lining does not correct this, but giving the patient progesterone will, and that is almost always the appropriate treatment. It can be given alone, in cyclic fashion along with estrogen, or in the convenient mixture of estrogen and progesterone found in birth-control pills.

The goal is to make the uterine lining mature normally, then slough off. If the hormonal treatment does not bring that about, then either there is a cause of bleeding the doctor has missed, or the lining of the uterus has been abnormally stimulated for so long that it simply bleeds on its own and will not respond to hormones. After many cycles in which only estrogen stimulated the lining, with no progesterone produced to act upon it, the endometrium may overgrow and develop something called hyperplasia. A D and C will diagnose this and allow subsequent hormonal treatment to restore the uterus to normal. If the lack of egg-and-progesterone production has caused infertility, drugs should be prescribed to make the ovaries ovulate normally. If ovulation is achieved, the uterus reestablishes a lining that cycles regularly and the patient is able to get pregnant. If the patient is not ovulating but doesn't want to get pregnant, birth-control pills will correct the bleeding, or drugs can be used to restore normal ovulation and the patient can use a barrier type of contraceptive.

Organic Causes of Bleeding

If the whole system is not straightened out by hormonal treatment, the problem does not involve the function of the reproductive system. Rather, the abnormality will be found in the structure of the system. It may be that the endometrium has become hyperplastic and unresponsive to hormones, or a tumor of some kind may be causing the problem. Both benign and malignant tumors of the ovary can cause abnormal hormone production, and they must be surgically removed. The gynecologist should be able to feel any of these on an examination. The benign tumors of the uterus described in Chapter Twenty-two, fibroid tumors, will cause abnormal bleeding if they are located just under the endometrial lining of the uterus.

In terms of frequency, most abnormal bleeding is of the dysfunctional type. After menopause there is normally a cessation of production of both estrogen and progesterone. The lining of the uterus dwindles to nothing and *no* bleeding should occur. Bleeding means either that the lining has become abnormal, and possibly cancerous, or that a tumor of the ovary (or, more rarely, of the pituitary gland or brain) has begun producing hormones and is causing the bleeding. That's why a D and C must be done in a bleeding postmenopausal woman. If the tissue itself is normal but has clearly been stimulated by estrogen production, the doctor must find out where that estrogen is coming from.

Endometrial Ablation

A new, still developing, and potentially very important type of treatment for bleeding problems is endometrial ablation. This involves one or more techniques to actually destroy the lining of the uterus. If the entire lining can be eliminated, there will be no bleeding with menses at all, and no cramping, yet hormonal production will be unaffected.

238

Currently, two types of instruments are used, the laser and an electrical instrument. In both cases, local anesthesia is administered and the instruments are passed into the uterus through the cervix. The basic techniques have only been applied since 1982, so long-term follow-up is not yet available. In fact, the procedure is not yet widely available, but is rapidly developing. It promises to become a major alternative to hysterectomy for abnormal bleeding, but a word of caution here. When doctors find themselves with alternatives to the procedures from which they derive much of their income, they generally find ways to use the alternatives to make up the loss. They do this either by doing the alternative procedure too often or by charging too much.

Questions About Bleeding Problems

If you see a gynecologist for abnormal bleeding of any kind, ask these questions:

1. Do you think you know what is causing the problem?
2. Is it dysfunctional or organic?
3. Do you have any reason to suspect cancer?
4. Will you treat me in the most conservative fashion and leave D and C, endometrial ablation, or any other surgery as a last resort?
5. Tell me what to expect as side effects of the treatment, how long it should take to get back to normal, and what kinds of bleeding I should expect during the treatment.
6. How will the treatment affect my future ability to become pregnant?

Twenty-nine

MENOPAUSE

EVEN THOUGH MANY WOMEN APPROACH THIS EVENT WITH DREAD, menopause is a normal condition and stage of life. With appropriate management, it need not be a miserable experience. On the average it occurs at age fifty, and it is simply the time at which a woman's ovaries cease production of the estrogen hormone. The lack of estrogen is reflected in a number of ways, because a number of tissues and organs are under the influence of estrogen during the reproductive years.

Even though menopause is a natural event, the symptoms that accompany it may be severe enough to consider instituting estrogen-replacement therapy. The pros and cons of giving women estrogen after their ovaries have stopped producing it have been debated for years. The same question exists if menopause is brought about by removal of the ovaries, rather than occurring naturally. Today the choice is clearer than it has ever been. For any individual, the benefits must be weighed against the possible side effects, and each woman must be considered separately and treated individually.

Hot flashes, or flushes, are the most common postmenopausal symptoms that make women consider taking estrogen. About 75 percent of women experience them at the time of menopause; 80 percent of those women continue to have them for a year, and 25 to 50 percent for longer than five years. These symptoms are harmless but so uncomfortable for many women that they strongly want relief. Estrogen administration reliably eliminates or decreases the severity of the symptoms.

The condition that poses the most significant health hazard resulting from lack of estrogen is osteoporosis, the greater than normal loss of calcium from bones. The loss of bone itself causes no symptoms; rather, the danger lies in the decrease of strength of the skeleton and the resultant increase in susceptibility to fractures. Over 250,000 elderly women experience hip fractures each year, 80 percent of which are related to osteoporosis. Other common fractures include those of the spinal column, arm, and leg.

There is good evidence that estrogen-replacement therapy can reduce bone loss and the risk of fractures if it is begun shortly after menopause. It is most effective when combined with exercise and calcium supplementation, and when given along with progesterone, as I will discuss later.

The vagina, being an estrogen-dependent tissue, will become thin and dry, and can develop itching, burning, discharge, bleeding, or pain with intercourse. Estrogen replacement will reliably alleviate those symptoms. The changes in skin that are associated with aging, however, have not, as of this writing, been proven to be positively affected by estrogen.

Although many psychiatric symptoms have been attributed to menopause, there is no evidence that lack of estrogen has direct psychologic effects. Menopause is, however, a psychologic milestone, and can obviously affect mood, self-image, and so on. Physical symptoms such as hot flashes and night sweats can cause lack of sleep, with subsequent emotional effects. There is no good evidence that estrogen replacement will have positive emotional effects, except as a result of the improvement of physical symptoms.

It is clear that women, prior to menopause, seem to have a protective effect from heart disease that is related to estrogen. There is an ongoing research effort to determine whether giving estrogen after menopause is worthwhile as protection against heart disease. In September 1991 the results of a ten-year study addressing this question were reported in the *New England Journal of Medicine.* This study, which involved nearly 50,000 nurses, was the largest and most convincing research to date. The researchers found that women who had been taking estrogen had half as many heart attacks and cardiovascular deaths as those who had not.

What are the reasons, then, *not* to give estrogen to postmenopausal women? Studies show that women given estrogen alone, after menopause or after removal of the ovaries, are at much greater risk for cancer of the lining of the uterus. This occurs even if low doses are given, and even if it is given cyclically, rather than continuously. It was long worried that the same might be true of breast cancer, but there is good evidence that taking estrogen after menopause increases the risk of developing breast cancer only slightly. To weigh all the factors, it is essential to know that heart disease is the leading cause of death in women, and that the rate is so high that even a small decrease resulting from taking estrogen would greatly overwhelm any risk from other effects of taking it.

The obvious conclusion is that women should take estrogen after menopause, but they should take it in such a way as to maximize the benefits and minimize the risk, and the regimen should be individualized for each woman. One of the keys to this lies in using estrogen in combination with another hormone, progesterone.

If the estrogen is not given alone, but is given along with progesterone in a cycle that mimics the normal menstrual cycle, there appears to be significantly less risk of negative effects and no decrease in the positive effects of estrogen-replacement therapy. In some postmenopausal women this combination may stimulate the lining of the uterus to begin bleeding again, and many of those women would rather accept menopausal symptoms than return to having menstrual periods.

In summary, all women who have reached menopause should see a gynecologist and consider the option of being treated with estrogen and progesterone. One exception would be those women who already have cancer of the breast or uterus. In those women, the treatment could actually stimulate the growth of the cancer. Regardless, every woman on estrogen-replacement therapy should be seen each year, have a yearly mammogram, and be given the lowest dose of hormones necessary to alleviate hot flashes and vaginal-dryness symptoms. Everyone agrees that women who need estrogen-replacement therapy and who have had their uterus removed should be given estrogen alone, not in combination with progesterone.

Finally, the most critical thing to know is that all estrogen-replacement therapy must be individualized, and this includes the decision whether to give anything as well as which hormones, in what fashion and in what combination, and for how long. Once you've started, stay in touch with your doctor and continuously evaluate whether you need to continue the treatment.

Thirty

PREMENSTRUAL SYNDROME (PMS)

PREMENSTRUAL SYNDROME, OR PMS, IS DEFINED AS THE CYCLIC occurrence of symptoms that are severe enough to interfere with some aspects of a woman's life and that appear with a consistent and predictable relationship to menses. Symptoms generally begin seven to ten days before menses and resolve within twenty-four hours of the onset of bleeding.

This disorder affects 30 to 40 percent of women in the reproductive age group, which means an estimated nine to twelve million women! It was first recognized as a separate entity in 1931. After fifty-six years of study, its cause remains obscure, and its treatment mostly unsuccessful.

In spite of a fifty-six-year history, PMS was not even accepted as a real entity by most of the gynecologists I know until clinics for the treatment of it began to be opened by women physicians, mental-health people, pharmacists, and nonmedical entrepreneurs. Even though there was still no clearly effective treatment for PMS, it was obvious that there was money to be made in the attempt. Gynecologists then began to start PMS programs and open clinics, usually owned by themselves but staffed by someone else. At least they now recognize that PMS exists, and many have stopped dealing with it in the worst possible way—that is, telling patients that their symptoms are psychiatric, not gyn, problems.

PMS is real, there is no doubt of that. Besides the fact that the specific cause is still unknown, it is a difficult disorder because it behaves so differently in different women. Included among the symptoms of PMS are irritability, mood swings, abdominal bloating, headaches, crying spells, depression, anger, breast tenderness, fatigue, acne, joint pain, constipation, incoordination, and craving for sweets, chocolate, or salt. The most common emotional symptom is the combination of anxiety, hostility, and depression, and the severity varies from barely noticeable to quite severe, including suicidal thoughts, violent behavior, paranoia, or panic attacks.

Gynecologists see women with this often disabling disorder every day. As a group, however, these doctors have had less to do with deepening the understanding of it than just about anyone. Unfortunately, the need for effective management has been so great that it has provoked a long history of poorly done research. This has led to erroneous beliefs about the effectiveness of specific treatments.

To illustrate the complexity of the problem, let me just list the things that have been, at one time or another, either suspected or postulated causes of PMS: estrogen, progesterone, prolactin, aldosterone, renin, vasopressin, endorphins, encephalins, melanocyte-stimulating hormones, glucocorticoids, androgens, insulin, melatonin, acetylcholine, vitamin B_6, magnesium, prostaglandins, and "psychiatric problems." There is no need for me to interpret all of these, because *none* of them has been proven to be the cause of PMS. It was always assumed that we at least knew that menstrual hormones were involved *somehow*. Recently, however, studies have given us reason to believe that they are not involved, at least not as the root cause. That is probably going to be found in the brain.

The list of treatments for PMS that have been tried or recommended is equally as long. Many studies have appeared to show good results for some of these at various times, but the hard fact is this: As of this writing, *no* treatment has been proven effective when studied competently, using placebos in a controlled setting. A recently published study suggests that a type of tranquilizer, alprazolam, can alleviate some of the emotional symptoms in many patients. This constitutes treatment of the symptoms, not the disease, which is where the only successes in the management of PMS have come.

Another recent study produced the very strong suggestion that treatment with a particular form of calcium was effective. The study has not been duplicated. Moreover, the form of calcium used is not generally available, so no action by patients is yet called for. It is a hopeful direction, however, and you will see more about it.

When the specific cause is determined there will be a specific treatment, and it will have an incredible impact on our society, for not only does PMS cause great suffering to a great many women but the effects spread through the home, family, and workplace, and the ill effects are vast.

It is my belief, as it is the belief of many others, that the cause of PMS will be found to be a substance produced in the brain that may or may not technically be a hormone. It may also be determined that some women have a problem handling some substance in the brain (like calcium ions), but until that is determined we must continue to treat the symptoms as well as possible. In fact, a lot can be done that *is* helpful.

The basic approach to PMS at the present time is, first, to determine what symptoms exist in a specific woman and to tailor the symptomatic treatment to her. Prior to any treatment, it is important and therapeutic to help the person understand all that is known about PMS, and to let her know that she is experiencing a real disorder, one that does not mean that she is an inadequate woman, a crazy person, or a hopeless and helpless victim.

Next, a PMS sufferer needs to adopt life-style changes and to eliminate the things we know to increase the severity of symptoms of the disorder. A good program includes a healthy diet, with an emphasis on complex carbohydrates, fish, poultry, and whole grains, and with limitation of salt, chocolate, caffeine, alcohol, saturated fats, and red meat. Tobacco should not be used by anyone, but PMS sufferers should be aware that studies have indicated an overall benefit in reducing PMS symptoms by the cessation of smoking.

Regular exercise has also been shown to be helpful in reducing symptoms, as has stress reduction, probably not by affecting PMS directly, but by reducing the overall background level of tension upon which PMS symptoms are projected.

Along with understanding that PMS is real, there has to be acceptance that it has real effects on feelings and behavior, and appropriate adaptation must be made. Know when in your cycle the symptoms are going to begin, and keep a calendar. Discuss with your family the effects that PMS has on you, listen to the effects your symptoms have on them, and try to conduct your life so as to minimize the impact of the disorder. Don't, for instance, try to confront major long-term issues during the worst part of your cycle, if it can be avoided. Ask your family to try to minimize stress in the household, and demands upon your patience and concentration, during the worst days of your cycle.

In addition to these general measures, there are medications that undoubtedly have positive effects on specific symptoms. Women who experience PMS primarily as fluid retention, bloating, and breast tenderness may get excellent results from a diuretic agent (spironolactone) taken from three days prior to the day symptoms usually begin until the day menses starts. Patients with severe emotional symptoms should ask a psychiatrist to prescribe the tranquilizer alprazolam on a trial basis, but only if there seems to be no way to personally adapt to the symptoms without this kind of help.

A number of other specific treatments are in common use, and even though studies may be unable to prove their effectiveness, individual patients report relief. I see no reason not to try substances that are not harmful, as long as the general measures described above are not neglected.

The use of vitamin B_6 is widespread; it is harmless unless the dosage is too high, in which case it can cause nerve damage. Don't take this without a physician's advice as to dose.

Drugs that inhibit prostaglandins (described in Chapter Twenty-six) have shown some usefulness, and if it is reasonable to take them regularly for menstrual cramps, I see no reason to avoid taking them for PMS symptoms as well. These are usually given two to four times a day when symptoms begin. Some of the prostaglandin inhibitors are prescription drugs, and have to be obtained through a physician; others can be bought over the counter.

Since many physicians will know little, and care less, about managing your PMS, I suggest that you look for a physician who is interested in its management, or for a clinic that treats only PMS. Beware, however, any physician or clinic that uses only one type of treatment for all patients, or claims to have a "cure" for PMS. As more is learned about the psychoactive substances produced in the brain, and their interaction with hormonal substances, a specific treatment will be found; but for now there is no cure for premenstrual syndrome.

EPILOGUE:
RESTRUCTURING
HEALTH CARE
IN AMERICA

WOMEN CAN DRAMATICALLY IMPROVE THEIR SITUATION BY CHANGING their relationships with doctors. They can support every woman who wants to be a provider of health care to women; take every opportunity to let male physicians, individually and collectively, know that their behavior must change; and make these doctors redefine themselves as males and bring a new sensitivity to their work. Every women's organization can demand change from the health-care system and from the government. Individually, each woman should approach her physician with reasonable skepticism and cynicism, and never again accept a doctor's authority without question. Women can begin all these things today.

Nonetheless, they will continue to receive inadequate medical care at the hands of the health-care system unless there is a significant restructuring of the way health care is financed and delivered in this country. The health and welfare of women is inextricably related to the structure of the entire system—to who pays for health care, who makes decisions about research, who designs insurance benefits, and how physicians are monitored. Because women get the worst of what is now a bad system, they can benefit the most from its reformation.

It is clear that the reform of health care is a top priority for a majority of Americans, and increasingly for the government as well. Most Americans tend to think of the problem only in terms of the cost of health insurance, without much understanding of the myriad factors involved in health-care cost, and without identifying the other elements of health care that are in dire need of change. Those in Congress look at the problem in the context of the national budget, and thus deal with such a broad overview that they fail to understand the elemental human factors that create the big picture.

Health-care experts tend to agree on what things need to be accomplished, even if they disagree on how to accomplish them. When the American consumer is questioned about deficiencies in health care and priorities for change, the answers reinforce the views of the experts. We all want essentially the same things.

We all agree that everyone in America should have access to adequate preventive medical care and treatment of illness.

We all agree that health care should be affordable, and that the cost should be made to remain steady in its relationship to other costs in our economic system.

We all agree that there should be a way of caring for the elderly and the chronically ill and disabled.

We all agree that the cost should be distributed in an equitable manner (but there is a tendency to think that "equitable" means that someone else should be paying for it).

How do we accomplish all this without sacrificing quality of care and while maintaining individual freedom of choice as much as possible? A number of proposals have been drafted by various individuals, agencies, and committees. Their conclusions and recommendations tend to reflect the biases of the interest groups that support them. It seems to me that none has proposed a truly comprehensive reform that will work in the real world.

Any potentially viable solution will have to change the dynamics of every element of the health-care system, maximizing the incentives for cost control and quality and minimizing the opportunity for waste, fraud, and abuse. Federal programs such as Medicare and Medicaid have tried to accomplish these things by simply limiting the amount of money paid to medical providers for everything they do. It hasn't worked, and it is time to scrap these programs and to replace them with a system that does work.

Countries that have health-care systems that cover virtually all of their citizens—Canada, France, Great Britain, and the former West Germany—have used various methods to contain costs, with various degrees of success. Those that have contained costs have done so with significant sacrifice of quality. The most common methods that have been used in these countries fall basically into one or more four categories. Some apply global budgeting, in which limits on total spending are established. Some limit the supply of health-care providers or medical equipment, such as CT scanners and hospitals. Some apply "utilization-review systems," which monitor the appropriateness of medical care provided. Cost sharing by citizens and government has been applied to a degree in France. This has been done in the United States; but other than this partial effort, however, the U.S. has completely failed to apply these programs on an effective, nationwide basis. All of the countries listed above provide health care for nearly 100 percent of their people for much less money than the United States spends to cover a much lower percentage. This is true whether you measure it by the percent of GNP spent on health care or the per capita dollars spent. Other countries do it better, but none of them does it as well as it could be done.

What I propose is not a Canadian system, or a British or French system, and especially not an American more-of-the-same system, but a new and uniquely American system that can use the best of what we already have. It would allow the government to do the things that it does best: that is, to collect and disperse money, supply regulatory oversight, and provide a genuinely nationwide system administered fairly to all Americans. It would also allow the private sector to do what it does best: control cost and quality through competition, compete through innovation and flexibility, and let profit incentives determine where there are areas of need that should be filled.

Prior to the development of HMOs, the cost of medical care was rising in an almost uncontrolled manner. The per capita cost of health care has tripled in the past five years, and we will spend a total of six hundred and seventy-five billion dollars this year and still get inadequate care. Competition and the normal economic market forces that arise from competition were not evident in the dynamics of the systems we had in place—i.e., indemnity insurance, Medicare, and Medicaid. By changing the relationships between third-party payers and doctors and hospitals, HMOs, PPOs (Preferred Provider Organizations), and other managed-care systems were able to dramatically change essential elements of the cost structure.

The most dramatic early example was in the area of the usage of hospital days. In 1983, the use of hospital days by members of Blue Cross plans was in the neighborhood of 700 days per 1,000 members per year. That means that for every 1,000 people enrolled in Blue Cross 700 days in the hospital were paid for, at an average cost per day of just under $500 (the good old days). In the same year, the rate for essentially the same-aged employed population in all HMOs in the country was about 400 (in my own HMO it was about 325). Even as early as 1982, then, HMOs were saving about $150,000 on hospital costs annually for every 1,000 people enrolled! Almost 40 percent of all health-care expenditures nationwide goes to hospitals: but remember that physicians control whether patients are put in hospitals, and how long they stay there.

As time went on, the gap widened between hospital costs in

and out of HMO systems, and the same level of savings was produced in the other areas of medical expenditure. This kind of difference was brought about by restructuring the incentives and motivations of physicians. Essentially, it meant getting them to eliminate unnecessary care, while providing all necessary care in the least costly setting for the best available price.

The managed health-care industry has instituted increasing levels of skill and increasingly sophisticated technology capable of bringing about saving. It is also now more capable of bringing these savings to bear while assuring quality and service. Not all managed-care systems have been effective, but the point is that cost control *can* be achieved by this kind of system. All it needs is the opportunity to apply proven techniques in a total environment that is supportive, and that gives everyone involved proper incentives to control administrative costs, assure quality of care, and compete on the basis of service. Here is how I would approach it.

I would direct all money that is now paid for basic insurance coverage to a federal trust that would act as the paying agency for a basic health-care package to be made available to every American. The sources of money would include employer contributions and state contributions, as well as all the revenues that now go to Medicare and Medicaid. Even though I believe that savings from the reform of the delivery system would be sufficient to provide coverage for the approximately 37 million people now without it, other sources of revenue could be developed if needed. They could include a value-added tax, a tax surcharge on insurance profits over a certain level, alcohol and tobacco taxes, and stop-loss insurance premiums from carriers.

Next, I would have a federal agency (new or existing) create a basic benefit package to be provided for every man, woman, and child. That package would emphasize preventive care and basic medical care, and would avoid such things as fringe practitioners and treatments, unproven therapies, and elective procedures like cosmetic surgery, hair transplants, and psychotherapy for personal growth.

This federal office would set the premium to be paid for each person based on age, sex, and locale, and determine differential copayments and deductibles based on financial status.

The same agency would qualify plans (HMOs, PPOs, insurance companies) to offer the basic coverage on an annual enrollment basis. Since this would be covering everyone, these plans could not exist without successfully enrolling members in large numbers, and would have to compete with the other qualified plans in the area on the basis of quality and service, not price. They would generate their profit by controlling costs, and they would do this by appropriately structuring their contracts with hospitals, physicians, and other providers. The plans would have the opportunity to restructure the ways physicians are paid so that the irrational differences in income between specialties could be made more equitable.

In addition to offering the basic coverage for everyone, the plans could offer supplemental coverage to individuals able to afford features beyond the basic.

The federal office, working with employers and state agencies, would issue vouchers to individuals and families that they would use to purchase the basic benefit package from the qualified plan of their choice each year. They could apply that voucher toward a more expensive expanded benefit package if they wished. On an ongoing basis, the federal office would monitor each plan's quality of care, medical treatment outcomes, patient satisfaction, and so on, and would be able to disqualify any plan that did not perform satisfactorily in those areas.

If all of the above was in place, additional state and federal programs could be initiated or altered to improve other areas of health care. The power implicit in the government's control of the money spent for everyone's basic coverage would allow it to shape many areas that need improvement.

It could give sanction to the use of providers other than M.D.s where appropriate. It could assure gender equity in the areas of physician reimbursement and medical research. It could give sanction to states to license alternative providers such as midwives, and to deny licensure to fringe practitioners who may be now licensed because of effective lobbying instead of effective skills and appropriate credentials.

It could empower state medical boards to access physicians' office records for review, require ongoing education and recertification exams for physicians, and instigate effective methods to investigate claims against physicians. It could mandate that states compile, and make public, information about every physician who is a provider for a qualified plan. Since virtually every physician would be providing services through one of the qualified plans, a lot more information would be compiled on an ongoing basis.

To alleviate the malpractice mess without sacrificing the opportunity for each individual to be compensated if they are a victim of substandard care, the new system should include mandatory arbitration of malpractice claims at the state level. This could provide equity both in terms of access to legal recourse and in terms of making the compensation consistent for similar levels of damage. The federal government could set standards for the selection of arbitration panels.

It goes without saying that we need further efforts to curb preventable disease at the national level, as well as legislation to protect against unwanted exposure to secondhand smoke, to prevent sales of tobacco products to minors, to control dumping of toxic wastes, and to alter many other areas where our own behavior, or our environment, is killing us.

If basic care is to be genuinely available to all Americans, the reforms I have described would still leave gaps in very small, very remote communities. We need, for this and other reasons, to revitalize the U.S. Public Health Service. With increased funding and increased authority, the PHS could be the focus for public education in health promotion and disease prevention. It could employ physicians to provide the services covered by the basic health plan in medically underserved areas by paying them enough to put them on a par with their colleagues who cluster in locales considered more attractive.

All of this is possible. It represents dramatic change, but change within the range of our existing resources. Physicians would experience the most dramatic differences, but only in areas that should be changed regardless of how we approach the finance issue. They have long enjoyed an inappropriate status, one that has not served us well. Whether we make the change rapidly, by government fiat, or slowly, by consumer pressure, we need a new style of physician in our future. We need a physician who is a skilled professional, paid at an appropriate level, and regarded with an appropriate degree of respect, nothing more and nothing less.

Our technology is of the highest quality. The changes we require are in the areas of social transformation, public policy, and the introduction of fair competition and ethical behavior in health care.

BIBLIOGRAPHY

Aaron, Henry J., and William B. Schwartz. *The Painful Prescription.* Washington, D.C.: The Brookings Institution, 1984.

American College of Obstetrics and Gynecology. *ACOG Committee Opinions.* 1981–1991.

——. *ACOG Technical Bulletins.* 1984–1991.

——. *Precis IV: An Update in Obstetrics and Gynecology.* 1990.

——. *ACOG Current Journal Review.* All issues 1991.

Blomqvist, Ake. *The Health Care Business.* British Columbia: The Fraser Institute, 1979.

Boyer, Ernest L. "Midwifery in America: A Profession Reaffirmed." Speech given May 13, 1990, to the American College of Nurse-Midwives at the 35th Annual Convention in Atlanta, Georgia. (Boyer is President of The Carnegie Foundation for the Advancement of Teaching in Princeton, New Jersey.)

Callahan, Daniel. *Setting Limits.* New York: Simon and Schuster, 1987.

Haverkamp A. D., M. Orleans, S. Langendoerfer, et al. "A Controlled Trial of the Differential Effects of Intrapartum Fetal Monitoring." *American Journal of Obstetrics and Gynecology* 134 (4):399–412, 1979.

Health Technology Case Study 37. *Nurse Practitioners, Physicians Assistants, and Certified Nurse-Midwives: A Policy Analysis.* Washington, D.C.: U.S. Government Printing Office, 1986.

Kaplan, Helen Singer, M.D., Ph.D. *The New Sex Therapy.* New York: Brunner/Mazel Publications in cooperation with Quadrangle, 1974.

King, Kathleen. Congressional Research Service—The Library of Congress. *Rationing Health Care.* July 12, 1990. CRS Report for Congress #90-346 EPW.

——. Congressional Research Service—The Library of Congress. *Health Care Expenditures and Prices.* Updated May 22, 1991 (archived). CRS Issue Brief #IB77066.

Kitzinger, Sheila, ed. *Midwife Challenge.* London: Pandora, 1989.

Masters, William, and Virginia Johnson. *Human Sexual Inadequacy.* New York: Bantam, 1981.

——. *Human Sexual Response.* New York: Random House, 1981.

——. *Masters and Johnson on Sex and Human Loving.* Boston: Little, Brown, 1986.

McMurray, Richard J., M.D. "Gender Disparities in Clinical Decision-Making." *American Medical Association Report of the Council on Ethical and Judicial Affairs.* Report B (I-90), adopted December 1990.

The National Commission to Prevent Infant Mortality. *Death Before Life: The Tragedy of Infant Mortality.* Washington, D.C.: U.S. Government Printing Office, August 1988.

Rooks, Judith P., Norman L. Weatherby, Eunice K. M. Ernst, et al. "Outcomes of Care in Birth Centers." *New England Journal of Medicine.* December 28, 1989.

Shoup, D., Dr. D. Mishell, Jr., B. L. Bopp and M. Fielding. "The Significance of Bleeding Patterns in Norplant Implant Users." Los Angeles: University of Southern California School of Medicine. *Obstetrics and Gynecology* 77:256–60, 1991.

Speert, Harold, M.D. *Obstetrics and Gynecology in America: A History.* Illinois: The American College of Obstetrics and Gynecology, 1980.

Starr, Paul. *The Social Transformation of American Medicine.* New York: Basic Books, 1982.

U.S. Congress. Congressional Budget Office. *Rising Health Care Costs: Causes, Implications, and Strategies.* April 1991. A CBO Study.

Wolfe, Sidney M., M.D. *Women's Health Alert.* Massachusetts: Addison-Wesley Publishing Company, Inc., 1990.